BLUESTONE MAGIC

A GUIDE TO THE PREHISTORY OF WEST WALES

Robin Heath

First Edition, June 2010

ISBN 978-0-9526151-0-1

Published by Bluestone Press, St Dogmaels, Cardigan
and printed by Gomer Press, Llandysul

This book is dedicated to 'the crew' of the Keewaydin

Bluestone: a geological group of igneous rocks, a type of basalt, the best known being dolerite. Spotted (*ophitic*) dolerite is bluish-green & flecked with feldspar crystals and was employed in various constructional phases at Stonehenge, some of these stones originating from the Preseli Mountains of West Wales.

Wikipedia

Magic: Enchantment, from the Greek μαγοσ, one of the Magi, an enchanter.

Oxford Etymological Dictionary

Magic: The Right Location, The Right Time, The Right Action, The Right Motive.

Sufism

BLUESTONE PRESS,

MEGALITHIC CULTURE

BLUESTONE MAGIC

A GUIDE TO THE PREHISTORY OF WEST WALES

Cover photo: The Bluestone outcrop, Carn Menyn, viewed from Bedd Arthur

ROBIN HEATH

author of

A Beginner's Guide to Stone Circles, "Sun, Moon & Earth"
& "Sun, Moon & Stonehenge"

Ramsey Island alignment

Copyrights

Carn Enoch

Want another copy for a friend?

For further copies of this book or for more detailed technical information about many of the sites described in this book, or details about other Bluestone Press publications, visit our website

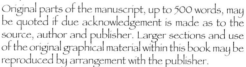

www.skyandlandscape.com

BLUESTONE MAGIC

A GUIDE TO THE PREHISTORY OF WEST WALES

CONTENTS

Acknowledgements

To my partner Trish, for her double-ended candle burning abilities, reading proofs and offering sound advice on this book late into many nights, my heartfelt thanks. And to John Powell & Emma Iveson for gently but persistently 'nudging' the project along.

An Alternative Look at the Megalithic Monuments of West Wales

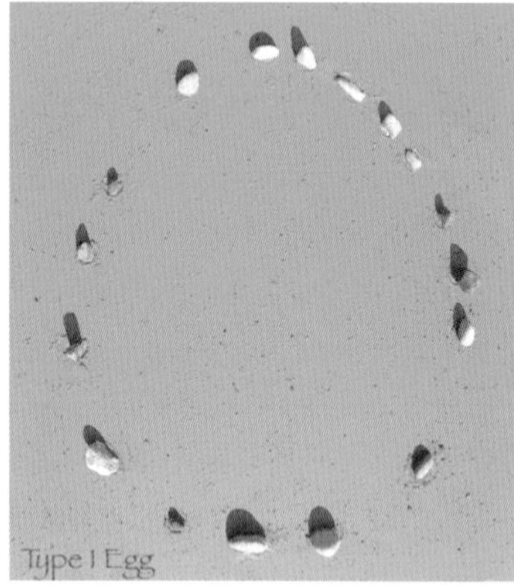
Type 1 Egg

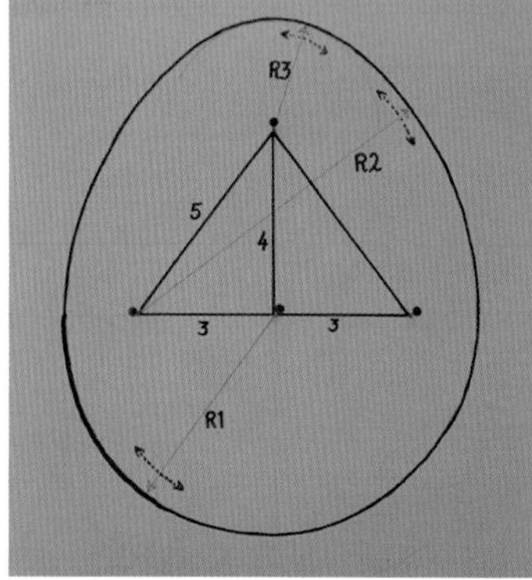

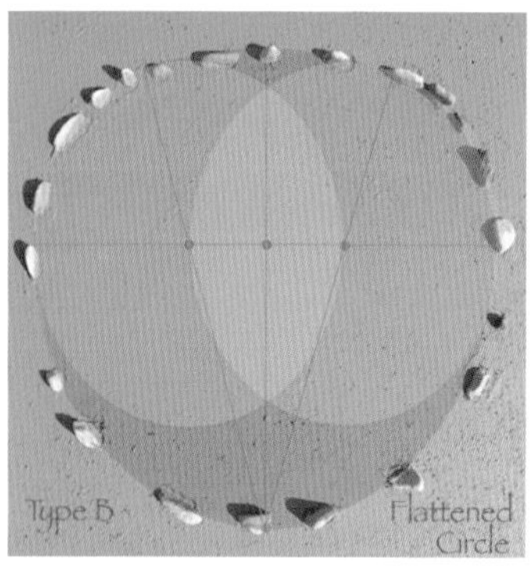
Type B Flattened Circle

Here is a story that has waited over 5,000 years to be told.
Have you ever felt, while visiting a megalithic monument, that there may be something more going on beyond the sparse model of human culture in prehistory presented by archaeologists and historians? If so, then this book may be exactly what you have been looking for - because it offers an explanation as to why those monuments are out there on the landscape, at a particular location.

This book is a guide to visiting the major and a few minor megalithic sites in the Preseli region of West Wales. It will tell you how to get to the site, and about the geometry (see left) of the site. It will inform you on how sites relate to others in the region, and how they are all related to their landscapes and skyscapes, for many of these sites do astonishingly interesting things with the sun and moon during important times in the calendar. And then there's some quite strange stuff to consider!

INTRODUCTION

Rising out of some of the oldest rocks in the world, the Preseli region of West Wales is home to an astonishing number of megalithic sites. Many of these have survived well the passage of time, enduring on the landscape over a period of between roughly four and six millenia. They were erected over a period that spanned over two thousand years, which began with the Neolithic period (roughly 4500 BC to 2500 BC) and which was all done by the middle of the Bronze Age (about 1500 BC).

Humans lived here much further back than this. Indeed they occupied this territory since the ice sheets melted during the Mesolithic period, but only during this single period of time did our ancestors engage in constructions involving unfeasibly large blocks of stone. This unique part of our history is often termed the Megalithic period, and until recently we have known almost nothing about why, when, how and why so many thousands of huge stones were transported and arranged as they were, forming an astonishing collection of monuments. This guide provides an alternative path to that taken by conventional archaeology in providing answers to some of these questions.

The monuments that stand proudly within that area of North Pembrokeshire that locals term 'Bluestone country' are often made from this extremely hard bluestone rock, known to geologists as dolerite. When polished it reveals a beautiful texture, especially when of the 'ophitic' (spotted) variety, where speckles of white quartz are distributed throughout the blue-green granite substrate. When polished it becomes very attractive, but the monuments here are not polished, and it is either to Stonehenge that we must turn to find polished and shaped examples of the

Preseli bluestone, some over 4 tons in weight, or to museums where highly polished bluestone axe-heads are displayed. In more recent times, a few local outlets sell polished bluestone pendants and jewelry.

The Preselis and their surrounding valleys provide an astonishingly beautiful and often wild landscape that forms the backbone of West Wales itself. While the Preselis remain central to this story into the mysteries and magic held within their rich landscapes, the boundaries of this guide book range over a much wider territory. I will be able to demonstrate that many of the key prehistoric monuments within these mountains not only form strong and previously undiscovered links to other parts of Wales and England, but that they also were employed within later cultural flowerings into quite recent times.

Pentre Ifan, Newport, framing the peak of Carningli on a fine April morning.

The representative monument of this region, Pentre Ifan (*above*), has become an iconic symbol of the Pembrokeshire National Park. According to modern archaeological dating techniques it is now thought to have been erected by our prehistoric ancestors around 3500 BC. It continues to be the most visited megalithic dolmen in Wales. This Neolithic 'horned' long cairn is located less than four miles from Carn Menyn, the famous outcrop in the Preseli mountains where, since 1923, geological evidence suggested that the bluestones were once 'quarried', from a tiny area around Carn Menyn, sometime before 3000 BC. Following their seemingly impossible journey to Stonehenge they would then play a central role within England's most famous megalithic construction. However, Pentre Ifan preceded the main constructional phase of Stonehenge by at least a thousand years, and this single, older, monument has come to symbolise the entire prehistoric past of the Preseli region.

The popularity the site enjoys today is not unwarranted neither is it a new phenomenon. In the eighteenth and nineteenth century Pentre Ifan had already become a 'must-see' for antiquarians and tourists alike, and there are a host of engravings depicting the monument, most of them fanciful, to be found in travel and history books from that period. Many eminent antiquarians, archaeologists and tomb raiders such as Sir Richard Colt-Hoare (1758-1838), Pembrokeshire's own Richard Fenton (1747 - 1821) and Wales's Glyn Daniel (1914-1986) visited the monument. Professor William Grimes undertook a full scale dig there in the 30s. More recently Professors Wainwright and Darvill have pronounced on it, just as all the rest in due turn pronounced on its possible purpose. None of them have seen the bigger picture to be described here, and there are remarkably simple reasons for this.

Prior to the adoption of the modern approach to site investigation originally proposed by William Flinders Petrie (1853-1942), archaeologists had previously resorted to pick-axe and shovel in a frequently futile and always destructive search for largely absent treasures they imagined to be found buried within them. In fact the real treasure turns out to be of a fundamentally different kind than those sought by artefact collectors, archaeologists and materialists, but this type of treasure has remained unrecognised and overlooked, even by the modern archaeological profession! The reader will discover this kind of evidence will arouse a different quality of interest than shards of pottery and the odd flint arrowhead. It tells of the forgotten cultural aspirations of our ancestors some three hundred generations back in time. The kind of evidence employed here has been ignored by the present generation of archaeologists and yet it reveals a great deal about the quality of thought possessed by the megalithic culture. What will be surprising will be the importance of their designs within the history of the development of the traditional arts - arithmetic & mathematics, astronomy, geometry and harmony. These subjects formed the quadrivium of a good classical Greek education, yet today many people find themselves lamentably lacking in an understanding of any of them!

Pentre Ifan is an easily accessed site located within the Parish of Newport and Nevern, in the coastal region of North Pembrokeshire. The monument attracts tens of thousands of visitors each year, who all come to marvel at this fine example of the megalith builder's art. The stone monument that one sees today is originally thought to have been covered with a huge rectangular earthen and stone mound, somewhat resembling a giant's sleeping bag, whose remains can be seen scattered on and around the lower ground to the north of the surviving stone skeleton of the monument. A display sign adjacent to the site depicts how archaeologists think the monument may have looked in its hey-day.

Visitors come and visitors go, in due season. Most spend perhaps twenty or thirty minutes at most at the site. If they are thoughtful folk they will ponder, as Henry James did at Stonehenge, on 'the enormous backdrop of time' and those uncomfortable questions that one must confront concerning one's own relative insignificance when faced with humanly designed and built artefacts from six millennia ago. Otherwise most leave with their photographs and a sense of having been there, to report back to their acquaintances that they have "Done Pentre Ifan" - seen the monument, and "Wasn't it an incredible thing that they could do such things in the Stone Age?" Which, of course, it was! But the thoughtful ones will in some way have connected with the past, and sensed the fleeting nature of a human life and thereby leave somewhat humbled.

Pentre Ifan - a Twenty Minute Marvel?

But hang on…just twenty or thirty minutes? And who were 'they' and how do we know of what 'they' were capable and just what exactly do we mean by the Stone Age? Primitive? What was the purpose of the monument and why was it built where it was built? How was it built? If you have ever gone beyond the twenty minute visit and pondered these bigger kinds of question, or felt rather strange goings on internally during your visit, then this is going to be your kind of guide book.

A further purpose in writing this guide book was to attempt to provide answers to some of the questions posited above. These answers reveal something of the real treasure contained in these monuments and this will suggest a much higher meaning and purpose for this and other megalithic remains scattered throughout the Preseli region of West Wales. It will hopefully also extend the visiting hours and future activities of the many visitors and tourists who come to wonder at these monuments. Pentre Ifan is seen to play a central role in these revelations, and in the later constructions of Stonehenge, a role which until now has escaped even the most inquiring and diligent of archaeologists.

Presently, the body responsible for cataloguing, preserving and maintaining the ancient monuments of Wales is CADW, (pronounced 'Kadoo'). CADW informs the Tourism Offices concerning what information is to be made available to visitors, in the form of attractive display boards adjacent to the sites, and within brochures and the other paraphernalia associated with tourism offices. This information is prepared by skilled archaeologists, most of it being a catalogue of the location of the site, its believed date of construction, its alleged purpose and the more modern history of the archaeologists who have visited (or plundered) it. Sprinkled like fairy dust on many of these bilingual display boards are the quaint legends and folklore associated with the site and, if one is fortunate, you may find a half-decent plan of the site.

On the surface, this practice works well. There stands the monument and, come the tourist or visitor, there stands the display board to deliver the presently believed date of construction, possible purpose and historical importance. However, there are several problems that arise from this approach. The first is that this present aid to tourism has demonstrably failed to lengthen the twenty minute stay, leaving much of the meaning of the monument unavailable. Secondly, the monument is viewed wholly disconnected from its landscape, to which it has been rooted for perhaps up to 6000 years, and thereby it is seen disconnected from the other monuments which surround it. This is completely non-holistic and it prevents a bigger picture of the monuments' relationships to each other being better appreciated. The third problem is that, presently, only a scattering of those sites which are considered more important warrant signage of this kind, while the other sites, considered of lesser importance, are largely left to the diligent and more determined megalith hunter to seek out within farmer's fields, hidden within gorse hedges or high up on bleak moorland. There is little and sometimes no information on the majority of these lesser sites, they are sometimes not even shown on modern maps, a void that carries some serious consequences for those keen to better understand the culture that erected all of these monuments.

In other words, our prehistoric heritage is selectively chosen, then wrapped up and presented as separate packages, completely divorced from any bigger scheme that may once have existed as an overarching development of the culture that originally built so many monuments in this region at such expense of toil. To give some idea of the extent of this endeavour, the present catalogue of those monuments that have survived the ravages of the centuries is over 400 pages long. It remains largely just a catalogue of locations, dates, often rough plans and details of archaeologically retrieved finds. There is very little in the way of connecting sites together or suggesting why so many individual monuments were built in the first place. Only the sites thought to be of prime importance are 'easy-access' and these are unfortunately presented as nouns and not verbs. The grammar and language of the builders' larger intent is left out of the script. Even worse, it is believed within the archaeology profession not to exist at all, a false belief I will demonstrate to be entirely unnecessary.

It is my primary aim that visitors who read this guide will be equipped to step inside the threshold of one of the many superb megalithic sites in this region and be drawn into an enchantment that spirits them away from the modern world and reconnects them with the ancient landscape and thereby to their prehistoric legacy. Some of those dots on the map, the individual sites, can be joined up, probably for the first time in thousands of years. Further exploration and questing into our heritage will thereby become an irresistible part of a visitor's stay. To enable this process, the criteria by which megalithic sites are evaluated will be enlarged, and the criteria of this needs some explanation.

Present day archaeology omits several vital components when it attempts to answer why these monuments were built. It does this because archaeologists are not trained to recognise these components. Retired archaeologist and stone circle authority Aubrey Burl goes further, calling this omission 'wilful prejudice' (personal communication to the author, 3rd October 2007). What are these missing components? That is the easy part to answer - they are the astronomical functions of many monuments and the geometry incorporated within their design and within their relationship to neighbouring sites. Were these missing components to be added, the implications for the present model of prehistoric society would be massive, and the conservatism and inertia within present day archaeologists has so far prevented acceptance of the inclusion of these missing components in any evaluation of the megaliths. The consequence of this has been that their model of prehistory remains two-dimensional, monochromatic and often vague, with remarkably few answers as to what the megalith builders were up to, nor why they built so many monuments over so many years.

If only one allows this evidence to be included in any assessment of the site, it is like switching on a rainbow searchlight in the dark. The sites come alive, they talk to each other, and they communicate much bigger truths than those relating to how or when they were built or how heavy the capstone is. We at last enter the minds of their builders and, as this happens, we break the sleep that has prevented our generation from waking up to the astonishing messages left strewn in our landscape by our forebears and left, whether intentionally or not, for future posterity. On this theme of intentionality, it is notable if not obvious that huge slabs of stone are inherently extremely hard to move and were therefore intended to endure.

To employ the word 'magic' in the title of a book about a subject that has previously 'belonged' almost exclusively to archaeology is, of course, to court ridicule from that profession. But I have quoted definitions of this misunderstood word in the frontispiece and perhaps use the word here more in the sense that science writer Arthur C Clarke used it, to wit, 'any sufficiently advanced technology that is misunderstood by the current cultural order tends to become regarded as magic'. That the megaliths remain largely misunderstood is self-evident if only from the failure of the archaeological profession to answer that most basic of questions concerning these structures - why were they ever erected in the first place? The 'magical' components have more relevance to the history of science and to parapsychology than to merely remain ignored by archaeology.

There are universal truths about being human and living on planet Earth within these monuments, and to the dismay of some archaeologists, the evidence here has the benefit of being easily comprehended by a non-specialist. Objectively verifiable, this evidence contains a scientific component that lends itself to the normal techniques and tools of scientific inquiry. Armed with little more than an Ordnance Survey map, a GPS device, pencil and ruler, everything I reveal within these pages may be verified. By you.

I therefore invite you be among the first people to take part in a new adventure concerning your past, everybody's past. The truth is truly out there, on the landscape – I can and will show you what some of these monuments are doing there, but it is you who must walk the land and you cannot satisfactorily 'try this at home'. The journey into the megalithic mind awaits your astonishment, here in West Wales, and it will demand a fair price – both during and after the journey you will find that much of your inner furniture moves around. The experience may change from visiting a prehistoric site to changing your life, as it did mine.

Robin Heath
St Dogmaels,
Summer Solstice, 2010

CARDIGAN BAY

N

MOUNTAIN PEAKS

DOLMENS

STANDING STONES

CAIRNS & MOUNDS

'CARN' OUTCROPS

STONE CIRCLES

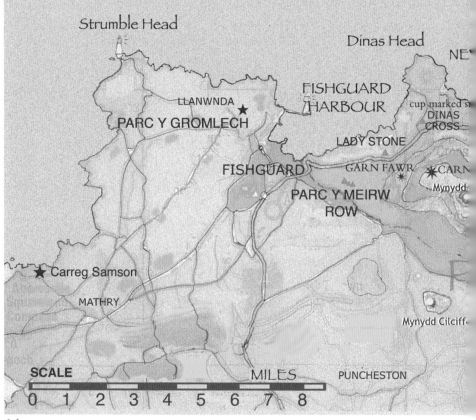

Strumble Head

Dinas Head

NE

FISHGUARD HARBOUR

LLANWNDA

PARC Y GROMLECH

cup marked s

DINAS CROSS

LADY STONE

FISHGUARD

GARN FAWR

CARN

Mynydd

PARC Y MEIRW ROW

Carreg Samson

MATHRY

Mynydd Cilciff

SCALE

MILES

PUNCHESTON

0 1 2 3 4 5 6 7 8

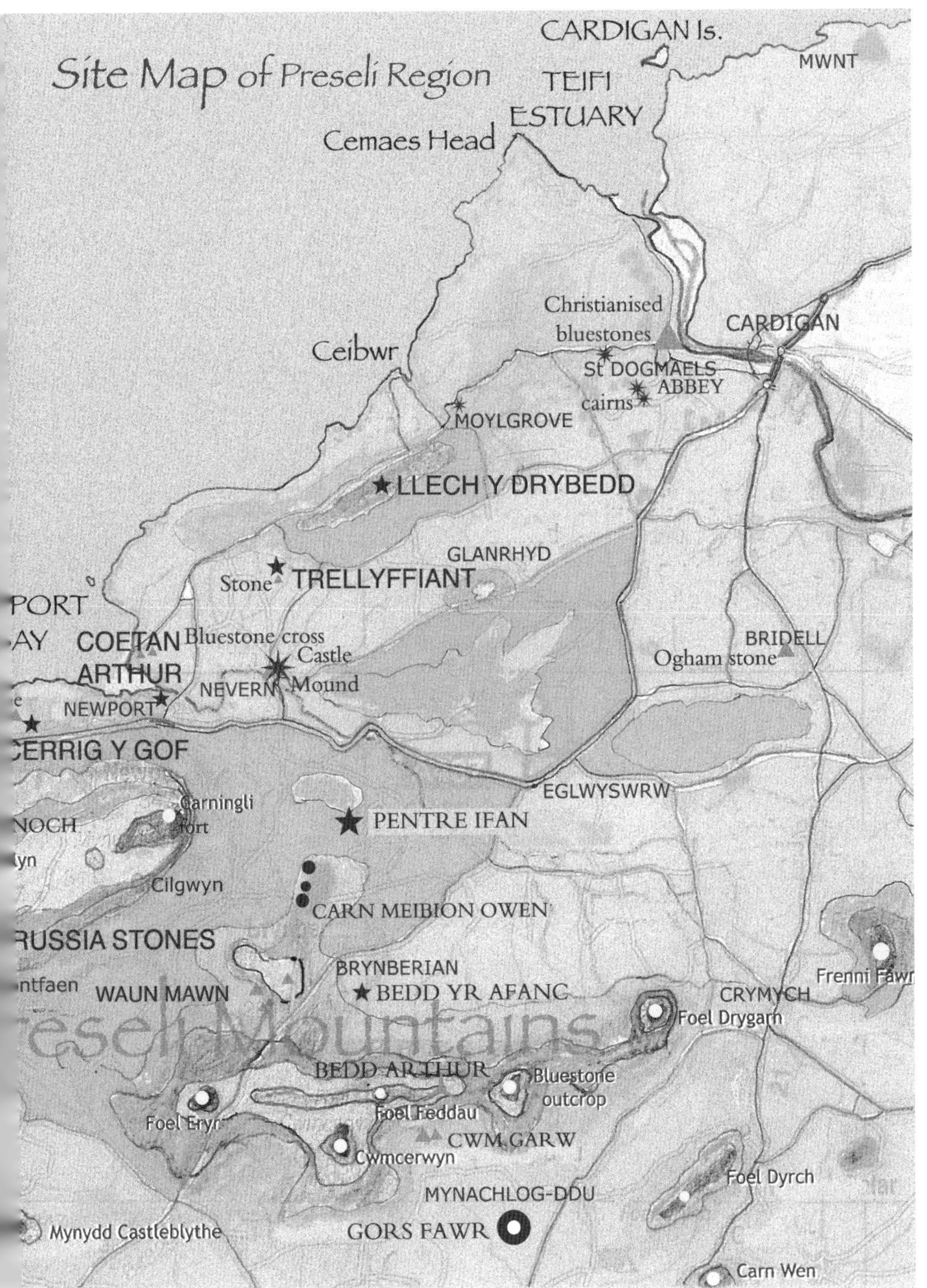
Site Map of Preseli Region
CARDIGAN Is.
MWNT
TEIFI
ESTUARY
Cemaes Head
Christianised
bluestones
CARDIGAN
Ceibwr
St DOGMAELS
ABBEY
cairns
MOYLGROVE
LLECH Y DRYBEDD
GLANRHYD
Stone
TRELLYFFIANT
PORT
COETAN
ARTHUR
Bluestone cross
Castle
Mound
NEVERN
BRIDELL
Ogham stone
NEWPORT
CERRIG Y GOF
EGLWYSWRW
Carningli
fort
PENTRE IFAN
Cilgwyn
CARN MEIBION OWEN
RUSSIA STONES
BRYNBERIAN
WAUN MAWN
BEDD YR AFANC
CRYMYCH
Frenni Fawr
Foel Drygarn
Preseli Mountains
BEDD ARTHUR
Bluestone
outcrop
Foel Feddau
Foel Eryr
CWM GARW
Cwmcerwyn
Foel Dyrch
MYNACHLOG-DDU
Mynydd Castleblythe
GORS FAWR
Carn Wen

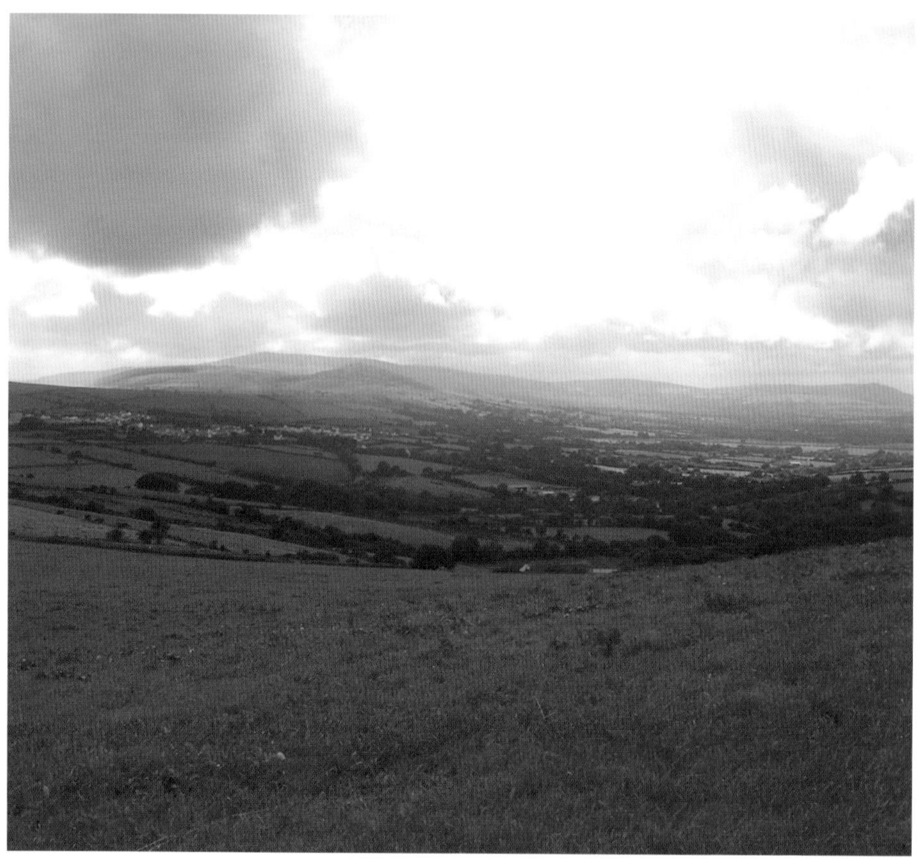

The two main Preseli ranges, viewed from the western summit of Frenni Fawr. From this leading and quite separate peak the remaining six peaks appear, with a little imagination, to resemble a giant coiled serpent whose head is marked by the triangular peak of Foel Drygarn, shown a little left of centre frame. The highest point of the Preselis, Cwmcerwyn, is seen to the left of this, while on the extreme right of this photograph is Carningli summit, eight miles away as the raven flies.

Chapter One

The Landscape

Discovering the Preseli Region

The Preseli Hills form the backbone of a large part of Pembrokeshire, and range from St Davids, in the extreme south-west of the county, to the small town of Cardigan, in the north-east. There are seven peaks in the main range, the highest of these is Cwmcerwyn, which stands some 1600 feet above sea-level. From East to West, these peaks and their surrounding territory are identified on the previous map. In the descriptive section that follows, the reader is guided through each one in turn, with the correct Welsh pronunciation. This oldest of European languages often changes the first letter of a word, a mutation that fits the rules of grammar. This charming quality of the language makes for confusing times when English people look up the meaning of Welsh words in an English-Welsh dictionary.

Frenni Fawr (pronounced Frenny Vower)

This high rounded hill is deceptively important as a landmark. Its name derives, as do so many Welsh names, from its function. Fawr is a mutation of Mawr, meaning big, great or large, while Frenni relates to the Welsh for queen, *brenhines*, making Frenni Fawr the Big Queen. Like the prow of the ship, which once often carried a female figurehead, this distinctive outlier hill leads the entire Preseli range. The summit is 1297 feet (395m) above sea-level.

Frenni Fawr can be seen from almost anywhere within the Preselis. The landscape appears to want us to see it, and sometimes important natural and built monuments are found to be placed in locations where it is just possible to see its rounded peak with two and sometimes three large tumuli visible on the horizon profile near the summit. Legends concerning the Roman emperor Maxen having set up camp on the summit are without evidence, the tumuli on the summit were found by archaeologist Richard Fenton to have been used for Bronze Age burials some 1500 years before any Romans trampled on these lands.

Sailing into Cardigan, once the largest port in West Wales, one keeps the prow of the boat directed towards the peak of Frenni Fawr, centrally placed in the valley that defines the river Teifi estuary.

It's a hard uphill walk from Penlan Uchaf (OS SN 212 345) to the summit, but the reward is a breathtaking panorama westwards along the spine of the main Preseli range (*shown on previous page*). The walk takes one past small wind-blasted oaks dwarved by the strong winds, and there are three ruined tumuli, well spaced from each other, lying along the the north-facing spine of the summit. In the photograph (*left*), taken from Foel Feddau, Frenni Fawr

Frenni Fawr and Foel Drygarn viewed from Foel Feddau

is the shallow cone-shaped hill left of centre. To its right and apparently underneath is Foel Drygarn. The reverse view, from Frenni Fawr, is shown on page sixteen.

Foel Drygarn (pronounced Voyel Dregarn)

Foel Drygarn (*shown snow-capped above*) translates into English as the hill or mountain of three cairns (Moel, mutates to Foel; Tre, meaning three, mutates to Dry, and carn, meaning cairn, is duly mutated to garn - it's complex, remember!). The name unsurprisingly derives from the three large cairns placed on the hill's summit, which stands some 1200 feet (366m) high. There is also an inconspicuous Ordnance Survey trig point tucked away on the northern side of these cairns.

Foel Drygarn marks the eastern start of the main range of peaks that defines the spine of the main Preseli range. It is distinctive because of its shape, rising almost in an even incline from its eastern boundary while its western boundary leads the eye onto the famous Preseli bluestone site. In certain lights and particularly early or late in the day or under snow or a low winter sun, the top half of the hill is seen to have been worked into a sequence of separate steps or even a spiral, and in this regard it somewhat resembles Glastonbury Tor. The snowy photograph above shows these features well. Over many millennia a great deal of human activity has clearly taken place on this hill, and archaeological evidence confirms that this peak played a significant role in the Iron Age community, so why not any earlier?

A walk along the Preseli 'top' can begin from the small lay-by at OS SN166 332. A farm track leads towards the peak and one gate later, changes in moorland vegetation indicate the pathway. There is a right turn to the summit of Foel Drygarn after a short walk, while the main path eventually, after about a mile, takes the walker up to the Preseli bluestone site, covered next.

The Preseli bluestone site, Carn Menyn (Carn Meini on modern OS maps). Looking east, the peak of Foel Drygarn, level with the far horizon. In the far right distance the summit of Frenni Fawr breaks the horizon profile. (photograph by Richard D Heath)

The Bluestone site - Carn Menyn

The high ground westwards from the summit of Foel Drygarn leads the eye along the horizon towards a highly noticeable rocky section. From many vantage points around the Preselis, silhouetted against the horizon it is possible to identify a 'craggy section' together with a large lump of rock that somewhat resembles a loaf or a huge saddle, the latter term from which its

Welsh name of Carngyfrwy derives. To the south and west of this distinctive feature, there are several craggy outcrops of rock, and the middle ones are the 'quarries' from whence the bluestones were extracted and thought by most archaeologists to have been taken to provide perhaps eighty-odd stones for the earliest phases of the monument we now call Stonehenge. Later these were apparently discarded, and later still around sixty of them were reused to form the smaller bluestone circle just within the vastly larger sarsen circle. Even later, still and further towards the central enclave at Stonehenge, nineteen slender and highly polished bluestones were placed in an incomplete elliptical shape which is now termed the bluestone horseshoe or ellipse. For reasons that will be discussed later, these stones from this site in West Wales formed an essential part of the most famous prehistoric structure in Britain.

The area around the bluestone outcrops provides a wonderful arena and a view that, on a clear day, is unparalleled. There is even a convenient level platform, the result of grinding glacial action over millenia, and this faces the long and magnificent southwards sweep of the landscape towards the Cleddau estuary, Milford Haven and Pembroke, while to the south one may be able to catch sight of Lundy Island, just over 50 miles distant in the Bristol Channel. Parts of the Gower peninsula are visible to the south-east, and to the east, the hills of the Brecon Beacons make a showing. To the west the coastal strip from Aberporth to Newport greets the eye, while going north one can enjoy a fine view over Cardigan Bay. Even on a difficult day, the magical atmosphere at this location never fails to reward the adventurous walker. For the really adventurous, try fitting a bluestone monolith into your backpack and taking it all the way to Stonehenge!

Following the rough path across a shallow 'v-notch' to the south-west of the bluestone outcrop there stands a summit which contains other outcrops, Carn Sîan (402m), and nearby can be found a second natural cairn, Carn Bica, together with a man-made and most unusual stone 'circle', called Bedd Arthur (Arthur's Grave). The monument is difficult to spot, as it is not on the skyline nor on the Golden Way path which traverses the entire spine of the Preseli mountains. The stones are rather small. Bedd Arthur lies below the path and to the south-east, and comprises sixteen small standing stones arranged in a boat shape whose axis is oriented towards the midsummer sunrise, near Foel Drygarn. Because the stones are diminuitive, several are now lying flat, and damage from itching sheep and mindless visitors have taken their toll on this structure within the past century. In 1985 it was possible to count eighteen stones. A photograph of this monument may be found on the first page of this book, with the bluestone site and Foel Drygarn in the background.

Foel Feddau (pronounced Voyel Fethheye)

Casting the eye further to the west the high horizon rises to a rounded peak, Foel Feddau. It stands 1531 feet high (467m). The name translates into English as the hill or mountain (Moel, as described above) of graves (Feddau, derived from the plural of Bedd, meaning grave). Right on the top of this rise may be found a remarkably large circular grass covered cairn, some seventy feet in diameter, on top of which may be found two symmetrical raised curved sections that resemble a *vesica piscis*, oriented north-south and about two feet high and twenty feet in length. These sections enclose a shallow

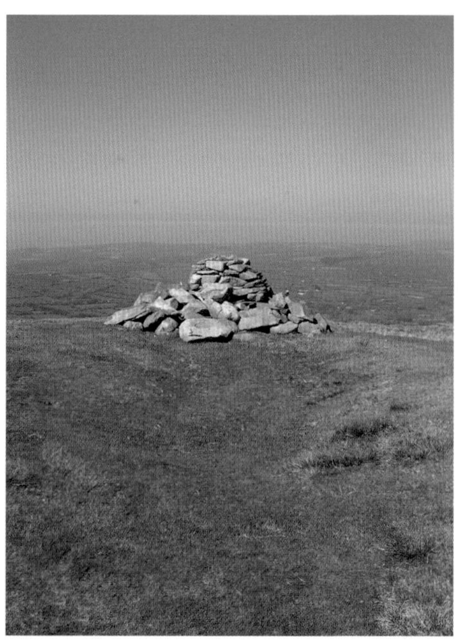

Looking north from Foel Feddau. The coastal ridge from Moylgrove to Newport lies below the sea horizon, in the middle distance is Carn Meibion Owen. The stone cairn is recent and lies on top of a huge grass covered cairn constructed in the Neolithic period. Over seventy feet in diameter, its top is sculpted into a vesica piscis.

depression, a sheltered enclave in the very centre of the monument. At the north end of this vulva shaped feature is a recently built rocky cairn, conical and about three feet high.

It is remarkable that after a few thousand years of being placed on the ridge of one of the most wind blasted places in Wales, the grass covering remains intact and healthy, while at Pentre Ifan, luxuriating in the verdant valley below, the years have seen all the covering stripped off. This fact begs interesting questions about the original form of these monuments.

Foel Feddau is a large and highly impressive monument, commanding an astonishing panorama over the entire Preseli range and across the local landscape both to the northwards coast, and the area to the south-east down to Carmarthen and Tenby. On a very clear day there are other things one can see. To the west there are 'islands', in reality two mountain peaks way across the Irish Sea. These are indeed Irish, being Mount Lugnaquilla in County, Wicklow, and Mount Leinster in County Leinster. These distances are not inconsiderable. Bardsey, a real island, is over fifty miles distant to the north, while Lugnaqilla is over ninety miles distant, as is Mount Leinster. It is a very lucky visitor who will see these small peaks rising from the sea horizon, but all are visible with the naked eye on a very clear day. We will revisit these three distant points later; they form an essential part of the story.

It is easy to imagine that the shallow depression within the *vesica piscis* shaped centre of the cairn would be an ideal place to place a cadaver, a place habited by hawks that would remove the flesh from the bones (a process known as excarnation) as part of the body's return into the natural environment from where it originally came. The practice of taking a corpse to high places for such processes to take place is suggested in Celtic historical texts, and Neolithic folk may well have held similar attitides towards rituals concerning death and resurrection. Once one recognises the *vesica piscis* at Foel Feddau as being a symbolic generative organ of Mother Earth, or the Earth Goddess, then returning a cadaver to its ultimate source becomes a perfectly natural and wholesome ritual connecting death and rebirth. Through its shape, Foel Feddau supports such a belief and may have been as spiritually important to its builders as a church is to believers today.

Looking southwards from Foel Feddau, as also from most of the other peaks in Preseli, it is possible on a good day to see another island, Lundy. At fifty miles range, Lundy is quite often shrouded in haze or sea-mist, but in the late evening, or at night, the lighthouse can commonly be seen flashing from the island, until recently from Beacon Hill, but now sadly replaced by an automatic 'light' at the southern tip of this island. A keen observer will also see another light flashing underneath it, one that takes a different rhythm. This second light comes from the lighthouse on Caldey Island, near Tenby, in the south of the County. An even keener observer will note that because the two flashing lights lie one above the other, that they form an alignment with the observer's location, this becoming exact in the area around Foel Drygarn, the Bluestone site and Carn Wen (*see page 35*). An astute map reader would note that this alignment appears to be almost precisely north-south, a fact that will assume increasing importance during the unfolding story of this book.

Like a reclining elephant, Cwmcerwyn, Preseli Top, viewed from Foel Feddau.

Foel Cwmcerwyn (pron. Voyel Cum Cerwin)

Cwmcerwyn is the highest point in the Preselis, standing 1760 feet above sea level (537m). There is a triangulation station (or trig point) on the top, and some small cairns nearby, helping those who travel in the lower worlds to identify the peak. These are just visible on the photograph (*opposite*). Set back a mile and a half (2 km) to the southwest of Foel Feddau, the peak appears much closer to Foel Feddau when viewed from the Newport to Cardigan side of the range. The view from the trig point encompasses the entire horizon. On a warm and sunny day and with not much wind it is a most pleasant pastime to enjoy matching the features and places shown on the OS map to what can be actually seen on the landscape, near and far. Good 7x 50 binoculars can greatly enhance this experience. From Foel Cwmcerwyn, walking westwards along the spine of the Preselis, it is, as they say, downhill all the way. Well, actually, not quite!

Foel Eryr (Pronounced Voyel Airear)

The pathway that tracks across the spine of the main range of the Preselis is an old, old trackway, sometimes called the Golden Way and more often the Drover's path. Only once does the modern world cut across it, in the form of the B4329 road connecting Haverfordwest in the south with Cardigan in the north. From Foel Cwmcerwyn, walking towards Foel Eryr, the older and hardly ever straight track meets the visitors car-park at Bwlch Gwynt, on the summit of the newer yet equally not straight modern road. It is unfortunately often a place of din and chaos, a rude re-entry into all things modern; litter, confusion about parking places and the odd boiling radiator when cars that have not been well-maintained make their ultimate steamy protest after climbing nearly a thousand feet in just under a mile. The crossing to the other side of the road can be tricky too, with large motorcycles sometimes racing over the top of the ridge from both sides, and also because the pedestrian path coincides with the entry into the car-park. Presently there is no speed limit to moderate the crazy dangers that can occur here, which also include stubborn sheep hell-bent on suicide, and the odd unruly dog.

Once the crossing of the main road has been safely undertaken, one is soon back within the tranquillity of the old Drover's track, aka the Golden Way, and the trek up to Foel Eryr. The path from Foel Feddau to Foel Eryr is shown below whose peak is clearly visible while the mad car park is not.

At 1535 feet high (468m), Foel Eryr (Eagle Mountain in English) is two hundred feet lower than Foel Cwmcerwyn, yet the view from the trig point is perhaps more impressive that that enjoyed from the higher point. To assist the visitor, a useful but incongruous etched stainless steel disc has been recently (1983) attached to the trig point. This indicates the direction of key landmarks, near and far, that are visible from the summit, together with their distance. There is also a large rocky cairn on the summit. Strangely, although it lies at the same height as Foel Feddau, this cairn has not a blade of grass anywhere to be found on its craggy surface.

In spring Painted Lady butterflies can sometimes be seen in numbers performing elaborate courtship rituals around the cairn, having flown in from North Africa to beautify our summer landscape. Other courtship rituals also take place here, on warm summer days when the air is charged with ozone and the scent of mountain grass and damp peat fills the nostrils. To serenade the lovers, skylarks rise up and down and treat those fortunate enough to be there to their warbling improvisations on a theme of skylark. If you are fortunate, the odd hare or three may display themselves, two even 'boxing' with a mate. And all of this real life is taking place only a mile or so from where folk remain resolutely entrenched within their parked cars poring over the Sunday papers and eating cheese sandwiches.

After Foel Eryr, the landscape slips away downwards and one enters a pause in the peaks and our journey explores a little detour. The northern route taken by the Cardigan road travels down a shallow valley - *bwlch* in Welsh - carved out by small streams on their way to join the river Nhyfer at Crosswell. A large smooth topped elongated hill lies on the far side of this valley, on the other side of which lies the beginnings of the Gwaun valley. At Tafarn y Bwlch, near the cattle grid, a path takes the rambler to some interesting standing stones, a pair and, further along the track, a splendid single six foot stone, called Waun Mawn, 'Peaty Track' (*upper right photograph on page 4*). To the north lie large fallen stones on Cnwc yr Hydd ('Outcrop of the Stag'). These may once have formed a very large stone circle, but now only three large stones remain and two of these lie recumbent. Further north still, this high ground finishes with the pyramidal rocky outcrops called Carn Meibion Owen, just to the south-west of Pentre Ifan. Local legend tells of three Owen brothers, who gave their lives defending their land against the onslaughts of English invaders. They are immortalised by these rocky outcrops, despite there being four of them!

Any further travels to farther hilltops involves crossing one of the most enchanting river valleys in the land.

The Gwaun Valley

The peaks of the Preselis are now interrupted by the presence of one of the most beautiful valleys in the whole of the land. The Gwaun valley (Cwm Gwaun), from which the town of Fishguard takes its Welsh name of Abergwaun, was born out of the waters of the river Gwaun, which, since the last Ice-Age, have inexorably worn away the softer rock that separates the main ridge of the Preselis from a second ridge. On a fine day a gentle cycle or motorcycle ride along the road that mirrors the river as it wends its way to Fishguard from Newport is an unforgettable experience. In April, the hedgerows are awash with Alyssum and Violets; in May, Bluebells and Cow Parsely; in June, Red Campion and Foxgloves; in July, Rose Bay Willowherb, while August brings this floral symphony to stunning climax with Toadflax, Thistles, Verbena and many other wildflowers.

September ushers in a mellow respite of blackberries, strawed grass and seed heads before the encroaching autumn and colder nights begin to nip and bite at the leaves, ushering in the reds, oranges, yellows, gold and even purple colours of the various trees that grow along the valley and flank its sides. Right until the end of October, a fine day will bring out the Red Admirals, Small Tortoiseshells, Peacocks and Comma butterflies to feast on over-ripe fruit, Michaelmas daisies and Sedum. It is all another reminder, were one needed, that this region remains profoundly beautiful, a very special place, a unique consequence of climate, landscape and the human history of the place. Much of this would have been as special to the men and women who were part of the communities that built those cairns high up in the nearby hills, whether to bury their dead, or to let the birds take the flesh off the bones for a later internment or cremation. And we often forget due to the archaeological obsession with digging, graves and death, that these ancient residents also lived and loved, as well as died, here.

No trip along the Gwaun valley is complete without a visit to what the locals know as Bessie's, but which the sign tells us is The Dyffryn Arms.

Bessie is the much cherished landlady of this most traditional public house, where even the future King is reputed to have enjoyed a pint or two. That said, Bessie makes absolutely no distinctions based on wealth or status and all are welcome to visit a real pub in a lovely spot and share some good yarns. And mine's a pint!

Carningli (pronounced as written) - 'Angel Mountain'

Across the Gwaun valley, and running parallel to the peaks already described, runs a second ridge, extending from Newport in the east to Fishguard in the west. Along this ridge can be found several notable peaks, but these are all much reduced in altitude from those lofty examples along the main ridge. Our first port of call is Carningli, easily the most easily recognised peak in the whole Preseli range, with a distinct rock strewn volcano shaped peak rising up in a steep conical form from the nearby flat ridge called Carningli Common, on its western side. On the eastern side, the mountain rises over 300 feet in just over a quarter of a mile, making an ascent on this side quite an arduous climb for the fainthearted or unfit, yet this is the main route up to the summit, which is 1138 (347m) high.

The shape of this mountain, visible from almost anywhere in the Preselis, even from Bardsey Island, is indeed due to volcanic activity. It is long extinct, visitors need not worry unless they are planning on staying a very long time. Over a hundred million years ago, a fissure in the Earth's crust ejected molten rock from this spot, and a lesser amount at cairns all along the ridge, at Carn Sefyll, Carn Enoch and Garn Fawr, at its western end. Many of the rocks at the summit of Carningli show layers from each successive lava flow, these strata resembling a grey chocolate layer cake, of a texture, age and most probably a flavour that one used to associated with cake served up at railway cafes.

Carningli is a superb vantage point, offering the visitor a spectacular panorama of the coastal landscape that leads from Cardigan and the Teifi estuary, to Dinas Head, Fishguard and beyond. There are great views of the main Preseli peaks from here, despite the peak being not much over one thousand feet high (347m). Walking up the ruined railway that was once used to transport quarried stone from the summit is a hard slog (*left*). However, this route runs by the side of an archaeological oddity, the remains of a Bronze Age fort near the summit, one of only two in Wales.

The popular name for this peak is Angel Mountain, after a Celtic Church saint, St Brynach, whose 'saint day' is the seventh of April. The story goes that this holy man was administered to by angels on the mountain, and reverence for this peak is upheld by modern spiritual seekers. St Brynach's church at nearby Nevern is an excellent place to plug into earth energies. This Holy hot-spot was important to the

Celtic Church of the fifth and sixth centuries AD, and as revealed later, long before then. There are several excellent local histories available at the church. A 15 foot carved bluestone cross (*left*), Ogham stones, standing stones and a beautiful atmosphere await you.

Carningli Common

Walking westwards from the summit brings the visitor to Carn Briw, an impressive but recently enhanced conical cairn some half a mile distant from the peak and the first of a large collection of prehistoric monuments strewn across the length and breadth of Carningli common. Here there are many hut circles almost invisible unless the light is just right or you walk right into them, and there is a famous large standing stone called Bedd Morus (Morris' Grave) sited at the Parish boundary on the only road crossing the common, from Newport to Pontfaen, in the Gwaun valley. There is a convenient car park situated here, and this is quite a good place to begin a walk eastwards to Carningli summit, which will take an hour forgetting stops to

Carn Briw

admire the views, megaliths and the wildlife. It also avoids the strenous climb previously mentioned.

To the west of this little car park there is a similar length walk to the long extinct volcanic outcrops of Carn Sefyll, Carn Enoch and Garn Fawr. On this side of the road there are many horses put out for summer grazing and many of these are white, such that a walker can enjoy being amongst the nearest thing to a herd of unicorns that it is possible to experience. In the right season, the lucky visitor may be blessed by the sight of a Fox moth, or even an Emperor moth, and when the heather is in bloom in late summer, it is often common to see hundreds of Red Admiral and Small Tortoiseshell butterflies feeding up here, with the occasional Peacock, Painted Lady or, if you are really lucky, a Clouded Yellow. There are views that take the breath away here - over Dinas Island and Fishguard Bay across to Ireland. Late in the day is best, when the sun is reflected on the water.

The first peak one reaches when walking westwards from Bedd Morus is the diminutive Mynydd Melyn (pronounced Minith Melin), at 1008 feet (307m). It is, in fact, downhill from the car park at Bedd Morus, which is just thirteen feet higher. But although Mynydd Melyn looks like a peak when observed from afar, largely a trick of the eye, it hardly warrants the title mountain (mynydd) or yellow (melyn). The visitor is forgiven for inquiring how the feature acquired its name, for there is apparently nothing about the site that warrants this curious title, and there is no record of it ever having been decked out with yellow flowers. More on this mystery later.

After Mynydd Melyn, the minor single-track road from Pontfaen to Dinas must be followed northwards, towards Carn Enoch, which is visible on the left of the road and about a mile away. For the unfit, frail or just plain lazy, it is possible to drive from the car park at Bedd Morus to a parking area near to Carn Enoch, and any OS map of the area will indicate the route to be taken.

The approach to Carn Enoch is a pleasant short walk, and the outcrop quite quickly becomes much larger than it first appeared. There are impressively huge slabs of granite involved in the original volcanic creation of this site, worn smooth by aeons of weather and the grinding action of a mile thick ice-sheet during several Ice-Ages. The vulcanism has left some interesting

Carn Enoch - A place of tally marks and magnetic reversals, where compass north becomes south.

effects to amuse the visitor. For instance, a climb up to the tip of Carn Enoch with a compass will reveal a strange phenomenon. At the very top the needle will swing around from pointing to magnetic north and point south, yet within a few feet it will swing back to normal again. This reversal of the magnetic field adjacent to the rocks at the peak of Carn Enoch (*left*) shows how the Earth's magnetic field has periodically reversed in distant times, the previous volcanic activity at the site having 'frozen' the reversed alignment of the magnetic material within the rock *in perpetuo*. There are several other places within the Preselis where this effect can be observed, but visitors can find the others for themselves!

Near the southeastern base of the outcrop, deeply engraved, are dozens of tally marks incised into the hard granite (*illustrated on the contents page*). Another mystery to consider. They are probably prehistoric and were certainly never carved there on a wet Sunday afternoon on a whim, yet they appear here, in the middle of nowhere carved on a huge granite slab apparently recording...*what?...nothing?*

From the top of Carn Enoch and looking almost directly east, through a niche between the higher ground of Carningli common, one can plainly see the summit of Frenni Fawr. Using binoculars, the reverse is possible, and Carn Enoch may be viewed looking west from the summit of Frenni Fawr. On a practical level, this could be seen as a natural arrangement which provides the only spot on the common where a beacon could be used to pass information backwards and forwards along the Preselis, from Carn Enoch to the northmost reigning hill, Frenni Fawr, the Big Queen. The alignment is usefully oriented, (roughly) towards equinox sunrises (viewed from Carn Enoch) or sunsets (viewed from Frenni Fawr).

The last remaining outcrop on this ridge is Garn Fawr ('Big Cairn'). It defines and almost stands on the very edge of the high plateau before it spills down into the Gwaun valley and Fishguard. This too is worth a climb, even without magnetic anomalies, for the view is simply splendid. From here, as for Carn Enoch, one can see the site of the stone row at Parc y Meirw ('field of the dead'), near Trellwyn, and the unusually shaped Poll Carn (156m), a natural rock feature near Great Trefgarne Mountain, near Wolfscastle, to the southwest.

This concludes our brief look at the two main ranges of peaks that comprise the Preseli mountains. However, scattered around these two main ridges may be seen other hills, sometimes as elevated and often impressive, yet not quite part of the main landscape. The casual walker without GPS or compass but equipped with the OS maps can identify these other peaks to assist navigation through the region while the experienced walker here will need none of these aids to get about.

Dinas and Strumble Head from Carningli Common

The Remaining Hills of the Preseli Range

The first of these peaks is part of a small ridge eastwards of the main Preseli range. On the A478 road southwards from Crymych, adjacent to and east of Foel Drygarn, a collection of hills stands out, their peaks being Crugiau Dwy, Foel Dyrch and, on the other side of the road, Carn Wen. The television mast for the whole region stands on the side of Crugiau Dwy (360m), and this mast is visible from most places in the Preselis, especially at night when its red warning lights form a vertical line leading the eye into the sky, and so often disappearing into the low cloud.

Foel Dyrch has a large cairn just under its summit (368m) and Carn Wen (289m) has a trigonometrical station mounted on its remarkably large flat summit, which is the size of two football pitches. Most of the north side of this hill has been quarried away to supply building stone, and presently there is no sign of the white cairn from which this hill once, presumably, obtained its name, for 'wen' is white in Welsh. But wen can also mean 'holy' or 'blessed'. A clue as to what happened to the top of this hill may be gleaned from the inordinate quantities of quartz boulders embedded into the walls of local chapels, farm drives and garden rockeries. Carn Wen forms a vital part of Preseli mystery and will be revisited later. For those who wish to visit the peak, you will need to clamber up from the A478 road side, the map now marks this route as 'right to roam'. There is a brick built 'powder shed' about a third of the way up, employed for the safe keeping of gelignite blasting 'candles', used in the quarrying. If you are a smoker it is probably not a good idea to light up near this shed!

There is a second smaller television mast within the Preseli region, south-west of the main ridge, near the tiny village of Woodstock, just off the B4329 and near Llys y Fran reservoir. This reservoir lies some four miles from Foel Eryr, and its little companion, Rosebush reservoir, is two miles nearer. Both lakes can be seen conspicuously glinting from many high spots in the southern parts of the Preselis, and together with the aerial mast these provide further aids to navigation for walkers.

Also to the south west of the main Preseli ridge may be found two other significant hills, both impressively large. Mynydd Castleblythe at 1138 feet (347m) high lies to to east of the town of Puncheston and within its parish. Mynydd Cilciffeth is some five miles south of Mynydd Melyn and Garn Fawr, and is 1164 feet (355 m) high. Both peaks have tumuli/cairns around their summits, and there are splendid panoramas to be enjoyed from either hilltop, especially of the islands off St Davids.

Finally, there is a most interesting ridge that runs almost parallel to the main Preseli range, from St Dogmaels in the north-east to Newport in the southwest. On one side is the coastal path and the sea, on the other are river valleys - Afon Nyfer and Teifi tributaries. At highest a little over 600 feet (185m), it contains a wealth of prehistoric treasures, many of them intervisible from the main Preseli range. Their story will be told in a later chapter.

This concludes a description of the territory that loosely defines the Preseli mountains. Should you wish to enjoy the delights of exploring this astonishingly rich landscape, you will at least need to equip yourself with the 1:25000 OS Outdoor Leisure Map 35 (North Pembrokeshire). A map is not the territory however and there are many places of outstanding interest, especially megalithic sites, ruined churches and significant holy wells that are no longer marked on maps, for reasons that escape common sense. Some of these sites will be described later, and in the bibliography there are books to assist locate and learn about many of these forgotten sites.

Finally, stay safe! Be aware that the height of some of this territory ensures that it can experience severe and suddenly changing mountain weather conditions, this demanding that suitable clothing, food, water and navigational equipment is packed up along with the map. Happy questing!

Chapter Two

The Sites

Discovering the Neolithic Landscape

In this chapter, the majority of sites that have survived in good condition and which are worth visiting are covered. These lie within a radius of ten miles of the bluestone outcrop of Carn Menyn. An OS grid reference is given for each site and a listing of the standing stones is given on page 51.

The Dolmens

There is no shortage of good surviving examples of dolmens in West Wales. Pentre Ifan is officially classified as 'a terminally chambered long cairn with parabolic forecourt', but essentially it is a dolmen. As the centrepiece of the entire collection of dolmens, sometimes referred to by archaeologists as being the principal member of The Newport Group of dolmens, it stands only a few miles from the bluestone outcrop. Other examples of this set include Llech y Drybedd, Coetan Arthur, Trellyffiant, the unique (for Wales) galleried grave Bedd yr Afanc, and the possibly Bronze Age and somewhat anomalous Carreg Atgof (Carreg y Gof). Coetan Arthur and Llech y Drybedd are quite similar in form and both are intervisible with Pentre Ifan. Trellyffiant is also intervisible, but even in its present rather ruinous state it appears to have been of quite different design.

There are other splendid dolmen sites just outside of the region covered in this book, such as Carreg Samson near Mathry (SM 839 337), Parc y Gromlech, Goodwick (SM 942 391) and Gwal y Filiast near Llanboidy (SN 171 256) together with some less well preserved monuments. Although outside the range of this present text these are all well described in a highly recommended guide book, *Neolithic Sites of Cardiganshire, Carmarthenshire and Pembrokeshire*, by George Children and George Nash. published in 1997 by Logaston Press (ISBN 1 873827 99 7). This is a very good guide indeed to the classical archaeological evidence, history and location of many important sites in these three counties that enclose and surround the bluestone region. Regrettably, there is no mention made of either the geometry or astronomical evidence at these sites, and the site plans are unrelated to their local landscape and sometimes inaccurately oriented.

The Newport Group

The local skyline for all this group is dominated by the presence of Carningli (*see earlier*), one of only two Bronze Age hillforts so far identified in Wales. Carn Ingli provides one of the most dominant topographical features on the local horizon, an easily identified focal point that is both ruggedly impressive and, when viewed from Llech y Drybedd, Trellyffiant or Coetan Arthur, pleasantly aesthetically symmetrical. However, many other peaks in the Preselis are also prominent from these locations: Frenni Fawr, Foel Drygarn, Preseli top and the ragged outcrops of Carn Meini, Carn Enoch and Carn Gawr are each distinctive hill-tops within the topology of the local Preseli landscape when viewed from all the coastal dolmens except Coetan Arthur and Carreg Atgof. The others afford some of the best views of the two Preseli ranges one will ever see (*see chapter one*).

Llech y Drybedd

(SN 104 432)

In Welsh, Llech y Drybedd means 'large slab on a tripod' (or trivet, *tribedd*), a most precise description of the form of this impressive neolithic monument. Located on a sweeping south-eastern slope on the Newport side of the tiny hamlet of Moylgrove in north Pembrokeshire, Llech y Drybedd forms one of a collection of portal dolmens whose largest and best known representative is the magnificent Pentre Ifan.

The Newport Group of Dolmens

The Newport Group and a friend. *Clockwise from top left: Low evening sun on* ***Pentre Ifan****;* ***Maen Corlan Samson*** *whose cup-marks runneth over;* ***Carreg y Gof*** *- a radial collection of mini-dolmens;* ***Trellyffiant*** *- 'Toad Hall';* ***Carreg Coetan Arthur****, in Newport itself;* ***Llech y Drybedd****, whose capstone closely mirrors Carningli when viewed from the right of the entrance stile (photographs of Pentre Ifan and Maen Corlan Samson courtesy of Professor Roger Earis).*

Llech y Drybedd is placed in a magnificent location, and it is best to choose a day with good visibility in order to fully appreciate the landscape vistas surrounding this site. These monuments, along with the many other capstoned tombs in West Wales, have long attracted archaeologists. Perhaps the first of these, Richard Fenton, described the site in 1803 as 'one of the most perfect of that species of druidical relics called Cromlech we have in the county'. Also of note, Grimes worked on these monuments in the mid thirties and again in the late fifties. Glyn Daniel undertook research with this group of sites in 1949 and again in the 1950's. Later research has been undertaken by Rodney Castleden (1992) and George Children and George Nash (1997). Further recent research and commentary has been made by Chris Tilley (1994), subsequently (2004) elaborated by Whittle and Cummings, prompting a very recent (2006) critical response in *Antiquity* by Andrew Fleming (2005).

Work on the prehistoric archaeology of West Wales is currently being undertaken by Timothy Darvil and Geoffrey Wainwright. Llech y Drybedd has therefore attracted many of the top names in the profession. Yet apart from cataloguing and preserving this monument, nothing much new concerning Llech y Drybedd has been gleaned over the years apart from a more accurate date for its construction, now given as sometime around 2800 BC, and that precision comes from the science of radiocarbon dating.

To date, however, no energy has been expended into investigating the astronomical significance of capstoned tombs, a serious omission that the author has been attempting to rectify since 1985. During this period both the location and the design of Llech y Drybedd was discovered to incorporate significant and phenomenally precise solar and lunar astronomical components. These properties are covered later, in chapter four. An alignment was revealed for both luminaries. This offers a significant contribution in understanding more fully the nature of the complex culture that erected this and other similar monuments.

Llech y Drybedd is approached from the Moylegrove to Newport road. About a mile from Moylgrove will be found a driveway on the left hand side of the road marked Penlan Farm. A small post indicates the footpath and now (2009) names the monument. A second left along the driveway after 200 yards, goes to the farm, and should be ignored. Instead continue straight on for 400 yards along a rough track to a left fork, which leads to a stile after 200 yards on the right directly adjacent to the monument.

The photograph opposite shows the 'saddle' between Cwmcerwen and Foel Eryr and the Carn Meibion Owen outcrops can be seen in the middle distance. The previous photograph on page 39 was taken a few feet from the stile, and shows the much publicised 'mirroring' of the capstone with the peak of Carningli.

Although presently balanced on three orthostats (upright stones), a fourth now rests recumbent and was apparently upright as late as 1693, still supporting the capstone. One Erasmus Sanders told landowner Edward Lluyd that the fourth stone was then in place. A fissure in the front orthostat has recently (1983) warranted a glass slide being riveted across the widening fissure (CADW), which has subsequently broken as the gap has widened. The capstone is also fissured. The top of the huge capstone is 2.5 metres (8 ft 8") from the base of the monument, and while little trace of a covering mound can be found at the site, extensive rocky debris lying under the monument and in nearby (10m) field boundaries suggests that such an additional structure was once part of the monument.

Llech y Drybedd performs other tasks than simply indicating a fabulous place to pause awhile and revel in one of the best views of the Preseli hills to be had anywhere in the region. In later chapters the monuments geodetic and astronomical properties will be revealed to indicate that this is amongst the most important megalithic constructions anywhere in Britain.

Trellyffiant

(SN 082 425)

In Welsh, *Llyffiant* is a toad, making Trellyffiant 'Toad Hall' or 'Toad settlement' (homestead). This odd monument, with its apparently fallen large capstone, is indeed toad like, and was once, according to Frances Lynch (1972), a double chambered tomb covered with an earthen mound. The second smaller capstone, if there ever had been one, is now unrecogniseable or missing. Originally Neolithic, it is possible to discern perhaps 35 cup-marks on the fallen larger capstone, this thought by archaeologist Glyn Daniel in the 1950s to suggest appropriation of the original site for a different function during the later Bronze Age. The Royal Commission for Historical and Ancient Monuments for Wales (RCHAMW) suggests that the marks are a natural feature.

However, just two miles to the south-east of the site a second large stone, perhaps also once a capstone belonging to a long fallen dolmen, may be inspected near to Dryslwyn farm. Here there may be seen perhaps 30 shallow depressions and these also resemble cup-marks, although the jury is still out on whether they form a man-made or are a natural pattern. An enormous recumbant stone, Maen Corlan Samson, in the field to the north-east of Pentre Ifan has two huge 'cup marks' placed like eyes on its western edge (*see page 39*), and on the western side of Newport, there is a fallen standing stone north-west of Cerrig y Gof (*see pages 86-87*) where large and evidently deliberate cup-marks have been incised into the stone. If the Trellyffiant marks are natural, perhaps the builders decided to show off their best decorative talents on the other sites, for there is no shortage of cup-marked sites in Preseli.

The name of this dumpy monument was evidently in use before the medieval Welsh historian Geraldus Cambrensis visited the site, for he recorded a legend that 'Toad Hall' was so named because a buried chieftain under the monument had been devoured by toads. Another local legend tells that the 'Toad' crawls off for a drink in the river Nyfer each and every Midsummer's Eve. Beyond stamping the site's name indelibly into the local collective consciousness, these legends tell us nothing about the monument's history nor intended purposes, nor why it is located where it is. However, it does connect the monument with a date - midsummer solstice - and this alerts us to a possible astronomical quality. Because we cannot be sure concerning the monument's original built form, it has proved impossible to ascertain any astronomical function that Trellyffiant may have once served.

To visit Trellyffiant, permission is required from the farmer at the nearby farm of the same name. At the time of writing this is Mr David Weston-Arnold, but will shortly be Mr Douglas Paterson.

In the field and about 800 feet to the south of the burial chamber(s) may be found an outlier stone, known as the 'Trellyffiant stone' (SN 083 423). In the trackway in front of this stone lies a large boulder that was once the top part of this stone. The location of both the chamber(s) and this stone form an important part of an unfolding story, to be told in a later chapter.

The Trellyffiant stone lies two hundred yards south of the Trellyffiant dolmen and stands about three foot high. The area around the stone and the dark grease on its edges show it to be much loved as a cattle rubbing stone. The piece missing from the top of the stone can be located in the trackway immediately beyond the fence behind the stone. The photo places Carningli directly behind the stone, to the south-west. The view from here is wonderful.

The Trellyffiant Stone

Carreg Coetan Arthur

(SN 060 393)

Carreg Coetan Arthur is perhaps the easiest site in Pembrokeshire to visit. It is located in a small enclosure within a small estate of modern houses on the northern outskirts of Newport. Of late, the 'Arthur' title has been dropped, a surprisingly bad move. Because King Arthur was thought by many to have been a Welsh king, the Arthurian brand name is good business for the tourist trade. Despite this, the signs now only say 'Carreg Coetan'.

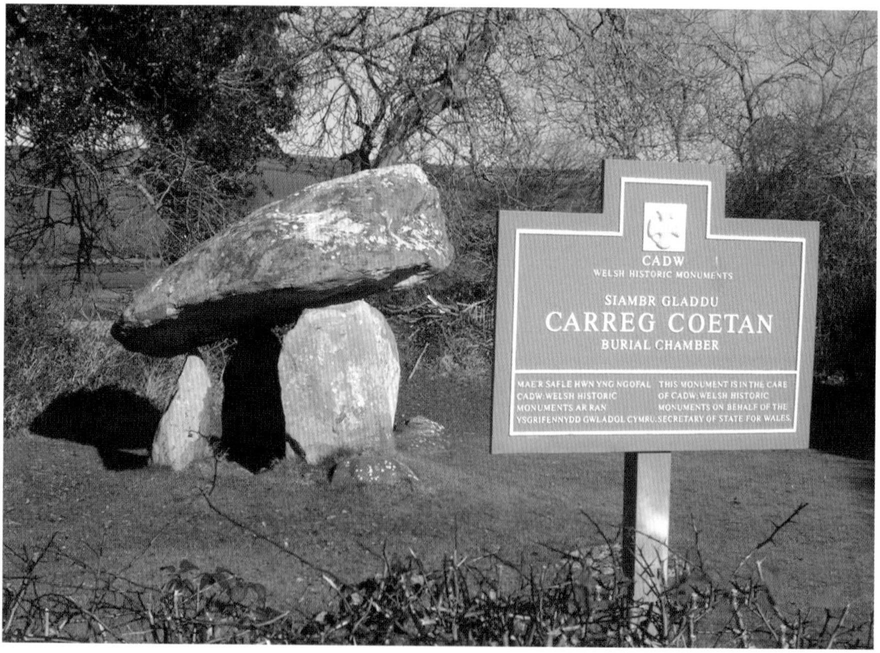

This dumpy dolmen has much in common with the design of both Llech y Drybedd, just up the back road to St Dogmaels, and Pentre Ifan, some two miles away. The two rear upright stones fit nicely into rebates ground into the capstone prior to assembly, which can be clearly inspected (*shown overleaf*). Take care to note while you undertake this task that the entire capstone now

rests on just two uprights, and even then only a few square inches of stone support its entire weight! Despite this alarming feature, which has stopped many a previously cocky visitor from daring to sit inside the chamber, the monument sits robustly looking out to the north-west, over Newport bay. Its axis is aligned to an impressive 'settlement' now a large semi-circular bank located near the estuarial path and adjacent to the town's tennis courts. This dolmen is almost on the beach, a few feet above modern sea level.

Visiting the dolmen could not be easier, by walking down from the town's main car park and along the estuary path until you meet the road bridge. Turn right and turn right again after about two hundred yards. The monument is well signed.

To the south of the monument the peak of Carningli and the smooth and rolling hill that is Carningli Common dominate the skyline. Although the tree cover somewhat restricts the views from the site, as do the modern bungalows, this small enclosure with its prehistoric dolmen feels rather good - a fine place to sit and ponder, or eat one's lunch, or even take a nap on a warm afternoon.

The site is surrounded by scattered stones that once belonged to a more complex structure around the monument. Coetan Arthur appears to sit on a small mound, but this has been shown to be plough-soil built up over many years, when land use was different here. Prior to this, the monument may have been about three feet taller than it appears today.

Carbon dating of charcoal found under a socket hole gave a date around 2700 BC. Cremated bone debris suggests that skeletons were only placed in the chamber after excarnation elsewhere - Newport Rugby Club perhaps?

Carreg y Gof

Cerrig y Gof

(SN 086 389)

Also referred to as Cerrig Atgof, this second name is probably the more accurate of the two, meaning 'stones of remembrance' or, literally 'memorial stones', rather than 'stones of the smith'. Whichever name one chooses, the site is very different from the other sites in this group, being a multiple burial chamber of radial design more akin to those found along the prehistoric Irish trade routes, and some multiple chamber tombs in both Ireland and Scotland. Both Daniel (1950) and Castleden (1992) suggest the design is a late innovation within the local group within Pembrokeshire, possibly belonging to the Bronze Age. It is sited within three miles of the suggested Bronze Age hillfort on Carningli, one of only two such sites in Wales. In 1811, Richard Fenton excavated the site to find charcoal, and very crude pottery fragments, some charred bones and many black sea pebbles. He was of the view that a central cromlech completed the radial complex, despite the central area being far too small to accommodate even a chamber similar in size to the rest.

Despite the ruinous state of Cerrig Atgof (*photo above*) the monument has a pleasing symmetry. The site is visible from the main A487 Newport to Fishguard road, just after Pont Newydd and on the right hand side. In 2009 a new gate was fitted to make access easier, so no more do you need to be a commando! However, the A487 road can be *very* dangerous at this location so park elsewhere and walk to the site with due care.

Evidence for the astronomical properties of the site and the function of the outlier cup-marked stone some 200m to the southwest of the monument are discussed in chapter four. Because Cerrig y Gof is dated much later than the rest, it suggests that astronomy was important well into the Bronze Age.

Bedd yr Afanc

(SN 108 346)

Popularly referred to as '*The Grave of the Monster*', a local legend tells of the monster being caught in a pond below Brynberian bridge and subsequently hauled up the hill by five or six horned oxen, to be buried with due religious solemnity. Afanc in Welsh can also mean beaver, perhaps a more likely title as none of the stones of this unique (in Wales) gallery grave would house a monster, as none stand more than three feet high. Because of their diminuitive size, archaeologist Jacquetta Hawkes described the site somewhat dismissively as 'hardly megalithic' as the stones failed to warrant their mega-status. The 'monster' lies in a flat bottomed boggy valley.

The photograph (*right*) shows the late Roger Worsley in full song conducting a guided tour in the early 90s. An enthusiastic supporter of the application of astronomy and geometry to megalithic structures, he opened the eyes of many tourists to the hidden functions of many sites in the Pembrokeshire National Park.

Bedd yr Afanc

The site was first excavated in 1938 by Professor William Grimes, who described it as 'an exceptional site in Wales'. Ten or eleven pairs of low uprights once led to a small circular chamber. The site is aligned roughly east-west on slightly raised ground within an often trecherous bog, requiring the visitor to don wellingtons and exercise extreme caution during and just after wet weather, which often means all year round in West Wales. Invite a companion along for extra security, or simply to assist in retrieving wellies stuck in the peaty bog!

Pentre Ifan

With Pentre Ifan (SN 099 370) we return to perhaps the best known dolmen in the whole of Wales. According to tourist evidence it is by far the most visited, requiring a recent extension to the parking facilities some 400 yards from the field, 'Samson's fold', in which the monument stands. There is good signage to the site, and it is easy to visit, with wheelchair access.

The magnificence of this monument is appreciated only by actually seeing it within its landscape. George Owen reckoned of the capstone that,'*The stones whereon this is laid are so high that a man on horseback may well ride under it without stooping.*' The height of the elegant capstone together with the crescent shaped facade in front of the entrance - the horned part of the horned chambered tomb archaeological description of the monument, make this site unique in Wales, and stamp it with features only to be found elsewhere at sites in south-west Scotland and Northern Ireland.

The entrance is blocked by a large stone wedged into the southern facade entrance. The door being locked, as it were, there is only a tiny and narrow gap by which to load the successive internments that archaeologists imagine were laid to rest there, for purposes largely mysterious. Some think that the bodies were added from the side of the chamber and it is suggested that possibly the cadavers or skeletons were discarnated (divided) prior to entry. All of this suggestion and surmise comes about because the acid nature of the soil and the wetness of the local environment has meant that no skeletons have actually ever been found, nor a trace of a burial, leading the major excavator, Prof Grimes, to suggest that cremation may have been the preferred ritual associated with the dead bodies of the elite tribal members placed within the chamber.

Despite all this uncertainty, Pentre Ifan remains confidently classified as a tomb! Other finds recovered from the excavation were paltry, comprising a

few shards of round bottom pots and some flints, including one triangular arrowhead. Thus the actual truth is that the monument itself is the only major artefact here, about all we have to work with is its location, its dimensions and its relationship to the surrounding landscape, while the archaeological evidence remains largely speculative. In a later chapter some reassuring astronomical and geodetic evidence attaches a new set of meanings to the monument.

Today there is little sign of the huge mound that once covered the monument. The surrounding fence gives some idea of the extent of this earthen and stone mound, possessing a footprint some 120 feet by 56 feet in area, and a height of perhaps 15 feet. Where it has gone remains a mystery, although if you were to stand on its summit, or the present capstone, you would enjoy a splendid view of the Preseli bluestone site to the south-east.

About 1,000 years after Pentre Ifan is thought to have been built, most archaeologists believe that Neolithic stone-acquirers were busy removing over eighty large stones from these bluestone outcrops around Carn Menyn and taking them off to Stonehenge. Why would they do that?

This concludes our brief look at the major dolmens found within the National Park region that have survived in good enough shape to identify their original form. There are scores of others, either ruinous or impossible to access or outside of the immediate Preseli region. Amongst these are innumerable cairns, tumuli and many sites such as 'forts' and *castells* which were perhaps built over earlier prehistoric sites. These may be identified from the OS map, and are for the more adventurous megalithomaniac.

The Standing Stones

In addition to the dolmens, the area in and around the Preselis is littered with other evidence of prehistoric life - the standing stones, stone circles, stone rows and occasional oddities that do not quite fit into an easily identifiable period or function. I have of necessity had to limit the following description to the major standing stones that lie within a ten mile radius of the bluestone outcrop. Most of these are indeed of bluestone, either dolorite or rhyolite igneous rock although the colour, quality and chemical composition varies by a considerable amount, reflected in the colour variation in the headings throughout this book!

In 'Bluestone country', the majority of the older farm gateposts are of bluestone, many clearly having once been standing stones, now irrevocably removed from their original positions having previously once served time within a different culture and taking a different function. Of very hard granite, these dolerite stones are more often than not of a greenish hue, especially when, as at Stonehenge, they are polished. The most spectacular of these stones are of spotted or *ophitic* dolerite, the greenish-blue granulated background composition studded with separate white flecks of quartz, the stone thereby resembling, with a little applied imagination, a star-studded night sky, augmented, in the author's case, by being quite short-sighted.

TABLE ONE

- The Preseli Standing Stones -

	Site	OS grid ref	Type	Distance (from Pentre Ifan)
1.	St Dogmaels Abbey	SN 1650 4580	6 Insc SS	6.7 miles
2.	Cwm Degwel (*not on OS*)	SN 1650 4545	SS	6.5 miles
3.	Bridell Church	SN 1765 4208	OghSS	5.8 miles
4.	Pantygarn	SN 1358 3790	SS	2.1 miles
5.	Dolaumaen	SN 1580 3113	SS	5.2 miles
6.	Gors Fawr	SN 1353 2953	2SS (aligned)	5.2 miles
7.	Glynsaithmaen	SN 1153 3053	SS	4.2 miles
8.	Eisteddfa Arthur	SN 1016 3575	SS	0.8 miles
9.	Gate	SN 1120 3023	SS(2)	5.1 miles
10.	Gate (north)	SN 1115 3035	SS	4.3 miles
11.	Temple Druid	SN 0968 2780	SS	6.4 miles
12.	Galchen Fach	SN 0978 2783	SS	5.8 miles
13.	Cnwc y Hydd	SN 0838 3404	SS (3 - circle?)	2.1 miles
14.	Waun Mawn	SN 0838 3404	SS	2.3 miles
15.	Tafarn y Bwlch	SN 0815 3370	SS (2)	2.4 miles
16.	Penlann Trehaith	SN 0803 3543	SS	1.2 miles
17.	Carn Meibion Owen	SN 0901 3575	SS (2)	1.0 miles
18.	Budloy	SN 0658 2855	SS	5.7 miles
19.	Fagwyr fran (West)	SN 0048 3146	SS	6.9 miles
20.	Gellifawr	SN 0641 3510	SS	2.5 miles
21.	Trellwyn fach	SN 0045 3560	SS	5.9 miles
22.	Trellwyn	SN 0011 3583	SS (2)	6.2 miles
23.	Parc y Meirw	SN 1998 2359	Stone row (5)	6.4 miles
24	Russia stones (*not on OS*)	SN 2034 2353	Stone row (3)	6.1 miles
25	Bedd Morus	SN 0381 3650	SS	3.9 miles
26	The 'Lady Stone'	SN 9955 3762	SS	6.7 miles
27	Dinas Cross	SN 0083 3885	SS	5.9 miles
28	Carn Llwyd	SN 0620 3785	SS	2.4 miles
29	Rhigian	SN 0396 3928	SS	4.0 miles
30	Newport Golf Club	SN 0560 4050	SS? (2 quartz)	3.5 miles
31	Clydach Bridge	SN 07083890	SS	2.1 miles
32.	The Trellyffant Stone	SN 0830 4230	SS	3.5 miles
33 (& 20)	Y Garreg Hir	SN 064 351	SS (9 foot)	2.0 miles
34	Penparcau	SN 091 354	SS	1.8 miles
35	Parc Lan	SN 090 358	SS (pair)	1.0 miles

There are gravestones, 'Christianized' stones and even lintels in ancient farmhouses that were once proud standing stones. In St Dogmaels Abbey there were many large bluestones that had been Christianized during the period of the early Celtic Church (around 300 - 900 AD), and four of these are now also wrenched from where they were found and posited somewhat incongruously facing each other within a modern information centre adjacent to the ruined Norman Abbey. All of which is to show that bluestone has provided, and continues to provide, an enduring stone suitable for ceremonial purposes since the Neolithic period. Polished bluestone is very attractive, even if it is the Devil's own work to smooth and polish it.

In the archaeologist's chronology, standing stones are thought to have been part of the later prehistoric period, and the stone circles and stone rows are often quoted as belonging to the transition period between the late Neolithic and the Bronze Age period (2000-1500 BC). We later provide evidence that this rule of thumb appears not to be be set in stone, and that acceptance of it can lead to anomalies in understanding the intent of prehistoric monument builders.

It remains clearly evident that there is an enormous range of size and quality of stone used in the construction of standing stones, stone circles and stone rows. In West Wales, the few surviving circles are nearly all comprised of rather diminuitive stones, whereas the separate and twin standing stones and the one well known stone row are impressively large, some over nine feet tall and weighing over 6 tons. In table one (*previous page*) every standing stone marked on the present OS Map and found within seven miles of Pentre Ifan has been listed, plus a few that are not shown on modern maps.

The Stone Rows

There are several impressive stone rows and linear banked structures to be found in the Preseli region, and not all of these are prehistoric. As a rule of thumb, the standing stones in the Preselis become larger towards the west and south. Some of the banked structures are the remnants of water run-off courses, presumably once constructed to assist drainage, while others are the bare skeletons of banked walls and field boundaries, animal 'runs'

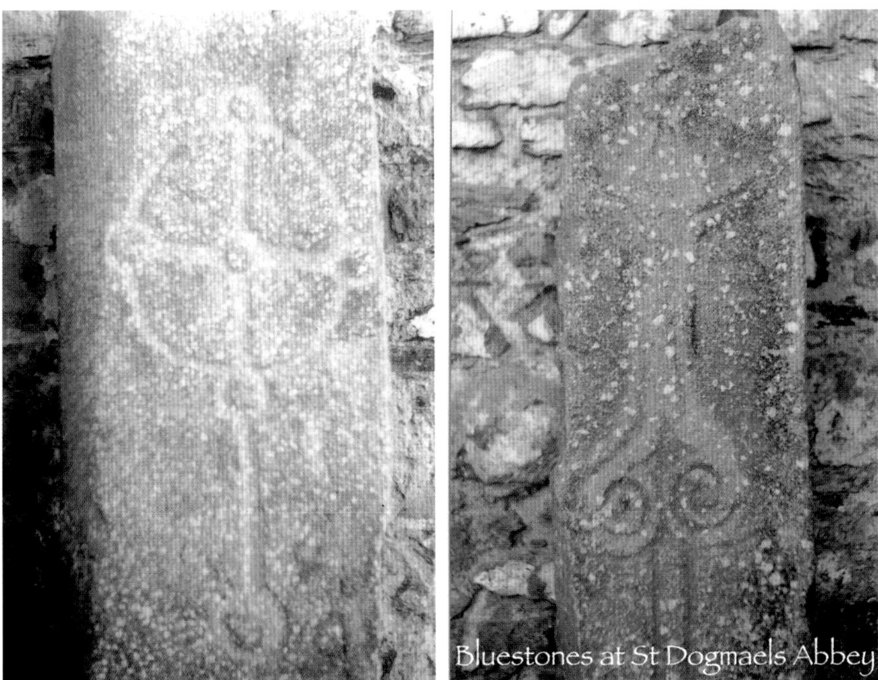

Christianized megaliths at St Dogmaels Abbey. Recently moved indoors to the new information centre, these are amongst the best examples of spotted dolerite in the land. Their original location may be lost, but these stones were clearly important long before the carvings were added. The design on the left is a familiar Christian icon, while the unusual design on the right is altogether different, and draws on earlier imagery and symbolism more of interest to earth mysteries enthusiasts and pagans.

and ancient house walls. We need not concern ourselves with any of these directly as other than incidental to the purpose of this book.

The surviving prehistoric stone rows of the region now exist as fragments of what may have once been more impressive monuments. The most famous of these is the row located two miles to the south-east of Fishguard. It was surveyed twice, by Professor Thom, in 1963 and 1965, and despite being buried in a ten foot high roadside bank, remains an impressive example of the megalith builder's art.

Parc y Meirw row

Parc y Meirw

(SN 998 359)

This stone row, whose name means 'Field of the Dead' in Welsh, is located on the left hand side of a single track road running from Mynydd Dinas to Llanychaer. On modern maps it is marked merely as 'standing stones' while older maps at least acknowledge that it forms a clear row of stones. There are other 'standing stones' marked in fields adjacent to Trellwyn farm.

The OS grid reference for Parc y Meirw is SN 998 359, and the site is difficult to locate visually, presently overgrown and obscured with ivy and brambles. There is parking of a kind for one vehicle as two stones from the row have been used as impressive gate posts for a field entrance on the left hand side of the road about three hundred yards from the farm as one proceeds downhill towards Llanychaer. It is essential to ask at the farm for permission to park in this entrance and/or to enter the field in order to inspect the true extent of this row.

The stones that comprise the row are enormous and more or less square in cross-section, although some have pointed or tapered tops. At an estimate, the larger stones weigh in at over five tons apiece. Most have their bulk concealed within the later structure of the bank that lines the road, but a thirteen foot long recumbent stone can be seen embedded within the bank further down the row from the upright stones. Parc y Meirw was clearly once a very significant site, but for what purposes? At present, the site is largely ignored by tourists and archaeologists alike, its scant details catalogued away in University libraries and its identity wrongly marked on maps. It deserves better, one feels. However, in the following chapters the site will be given a fresh airing, and may enjoy a less neglected future.

In a field west of Trellwyn farm may be found two more stones, much smaller but possibly once part of a continuous row, visible from the road. One stone lies against a hedge. Also visible from the road just west of Trellwyn Fach is a single standing stone, which is clearly unaligned with the extended row. One feels this location holds more secrets from the past.

STONE ROW - RUSSIA (SN 2034 2353)

The Russia Stones

(SN 023 353)

Near a hair-pin bend on the road from Dinas to the Gwaun Valley are three massive standing stones. Two of them make up the most ostentatious pair of gateposts in Pembrokeshire, while a third lies to the East about a hundred yards distant, also now downgraded to a gatepost. Essentially all three are bluestones of the same type, shape and size as those stones which make up the Parc y Meirw alignment, located about a mile and a half distant,

in Russia, that curiously named place marked on the map and strewn with glacial erratics - large boulders - heaped into field boundaries. Experience has taught me that it is the often biting wind here that gives rise to the curious name of this location.

Although now comprising of only three upright stones, there are other massive stones lying recumbent in the banked field boundary. The collection is so similar to those of Parc y Meirw that an assumption that they were erected by the same culture who built Parc y Meirw would be a reasonable one. Impressively large bluestones become more interesting when one discovers that the row is accurately aligned East-West, which is very unlikely to have occurred by chance. The lower illustrations show the view from stone 1, the right hand image 'shot' through the theodolite eyepiece. The astronomical qualities of sites are discussed further in chapter four.

The Stone Circles

The Preseli region does not fare well when it comes to surviving stone circles. Older maps reveal that during the past two centuries no little destruction has been unleashed on what were once the largest stone circles in this part of Wales. As for some of the standing stones that now are mere stumps, the culprits were anti-pagan Christians and/or farmers, both groups using large horses and later dynamite and tractors to reduce our most ancient heritage to building stone, gateposts and ragged debris. The dynamite drilling 'fingers' can be seen along the resulting fissure on many stumps. Like some grotesque parody of the Ogham script these eloquently confirm the recent destruction.

What few circles survive are small both in size and their perimeters have been defined using rather small stones. Visually they are not as impressive as the rings to be found in other beautiful and remote areas of Britain, like the Lake District and Cornwall. But they are interesting and they share many of the features of their larger cousins.

The best known of the Preseli circles is **Gors Fawr**, very nearly a true circle and located just below the Bluestone outcrop on the boggy plain on the south side of Carn Menyn. Its name translates, literally if not very invitingly to 'big bog' . Over the centuries, year on year, the height of this bog has been increasing so that today most of the length of the stones lies buried.

Gors Fawr is splendidly located within a landscape that uncannily resembles the backdrop to the Apollo lunar landing films taken by astronauts in the late 1960s and early 70s. This is especially true at night time under a strong moon. The site is well worth a visit at any time; evocative and mysterious, it connects the visitor to the ancestors in a remarkably effective manner. Wear wellingtons or really good boots, and cross the stile found about a mile and a half along the minor road that leads from Mynachlog-ddu

to Maenclochog. There is one of Pembrokeshire's classic bungalows to the north of the site, made from corrugated iron (known as 'wriggly tin' in these parts) and, this, plus the old rusty sign and matching 1950s stile provided, until quite recently, an evocative retro vibe. (*see photograph on previous page*). The site is less than four hundred yards from the road across a flat, boggy, acid-soiled moorland. From Mynachlog-ddu take the road to Llangolmen, Gors Fawr is on the right after about a mile and well signed.

The circle comprises sixteen stones whose largest members lie on the southern side of the ring. A complicated and not-understood central area contains what may be recumbent stones. Hippies and other alternative people have lit fires and held ceremonies in this ring for forty years, so that sometimes one can find various items of modern tat surrounding these cremations for sundry beliefs and peculiar causes.

Gors Fawr

While at the site it is worth identifying certain points on the distant horizon where there can be seen cairns, notches and other noticeable features right on the skyline. Some of these are rumoured to hold astronomical alignments to key moments in the calendar or lunar cycle, an aspect of megalithic sites to be explored in a later section.

To the north of the ring may be found two much larger outlier stones, and these are aligned so that the gap between them indicates the position of the rising midsummer sun on the horizon. The rear stone of the pair is shaped somewhat like a high backed chair, and provides a tolerable seat.

The surrounding bog is littered with interesting and often huge stones such that the visitor can imagine without much effort that a huge lost city once stood on this site. More realistically, the site is covered in leftovers from the melting glacial ice sheets, from a few millenia before Gors Fawr appeared. The Carn Menyn outcrop is due north of here and the famous Stonehenge bluestones almost certainly passed over this boggy plain at some time in the prehistoric past, whether carried by ice or by the strong arms of very ambitious Neolithic architects for reasons yet to be discussed.

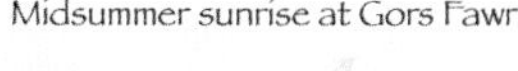

Midsummer sunrise at Gors Fawr

Meini Gwyr

(SN 041 266)

In her excellent book *Prehistoric Preseli*, Archaeologist Dr Figgis says of Meini Gwyr that it has '..*something of the henge, something of the stone circle and something of the ring-barrow in its design*'. The scholarly reconstruction resembles the early design of Bryn Celli Ddu, on Anglesey, a site which also had its passage aligned to the midsummer sunrise. If the archaeological reconstruction of this site is even half accurate, then this was a highly significant site for the community that once populated the area around Glandy Cross, described, again by 'Paddy' Figgis, as '*the least known and most important gathering of ritual sites in West Wales*'. The dating of some of the radiocarbon samples

Meini Gwyr

has given dates of 4300 BC, which is right at the presumed start of the Neolithic period. This fits with the sea-routes along the West Wales coast known to have been used by early neolithic traders, and agrees with samples evaluated from Bryn Celli Ddu.

All that remains of Meini Gwyr today is a circular raised bank and two surviving stones opposite a local cricket club. The centres of the other fifteen stones, which were apparently all leaning inwards, were identified and marked with concrete plugs, these have since been ripped out and dumped under a nearby hedge.

Two fields to the west of Meini Gwyr stand two other standing stones, Yr Allor, although three stood in living memory. Archaeologists have describe these as a 'Cove', as found at Avebury and Stanton Drew circles. Early descriptions of the Preseli monuments suggest that another large stone circle existed here - it is even marked on some antiquarian maps.

Along the road that wends its way to Mynchlog-ddu from Glandy Cross, about 400 yards from the five way crossroads, a small stone circle may be discovered some 300 yards from a farm gate on the right of the road (permission is need to walk across the field). The stones are very small, but a theodolite survey in 2001 revealed that the design was not circular, the geometry being that of what is termed a 'type B' flattened circle (*see diagram at bottom left of page 4*). On the map of Glandy Cross complex shown opposite, it is shown as a kerbed cairn, although there is no sign of the cairn anymore, and the circle is cut into two by a high banked field boundary. Enough remains to determine the geometry, whose centre is unusual in that it is marked by a stone. The 'circle' were it not flattened would be 28 feet in radius. The view here is wonderful, even if the stone ring is spoiled.

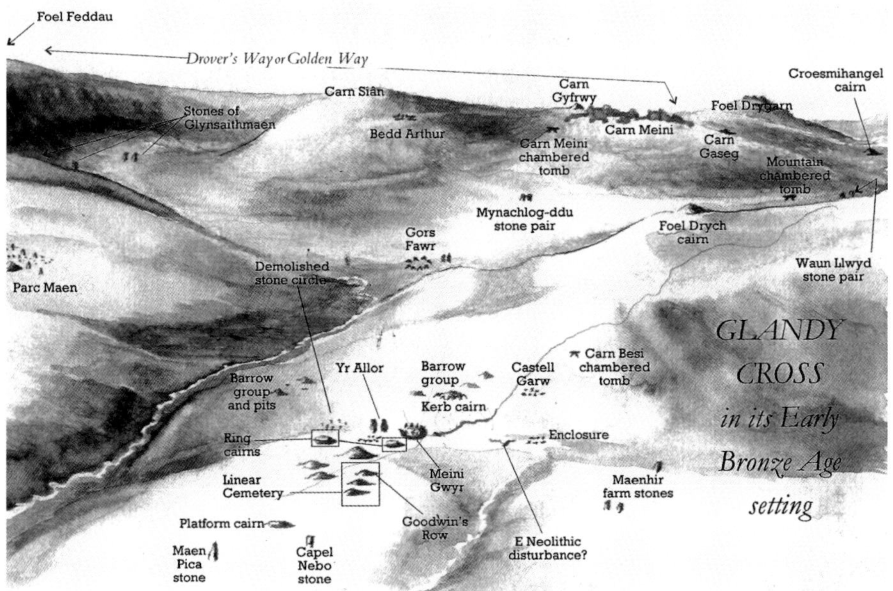

The Glandy Cross Complex is one of the most important prehistoric sites in Western Britain. The map shows something of what was once an immensely important cultural centre, just three miles from the bluestone outcrop (courtesy Dr N P Figgis).

Bedd Arthur

(SN 132 325)

Also shown on the above map is a most interesting boat-shaped stone ring called Bedd Arthur - Arthur's Grave (*see photograph on page 1 and location details on page 21-22*). Now made up of sixteen stones, their size may be diminutive, but the monument's axis packs an interesting punch, locating the position of midsummer sunrise during the Neolithic period - at about 47° east of north, depending on the horizon elevation. Someone during these distant times was very interested in the midsummer sunrise position, yet you will find no mention of this in any of the normal literature about these monuments, nor other astronomical or geometrical details about any of the sites itemised in this book. Time to rectify matters, perhaps?

Bedd Arthur (Arthur's Grave). This unusual boat shaped monument lies just over half a mile from the bluestone outcrop of Carn Menyn. A theodolite survey reveals its axis is aligned to the midsummer sunrise as would have been observed around 2500 BC. To the right is Foel Drygarn and, behind that, Frenni Fawr.

Brithdir Mawr

Within the past twelve years, an alleged one-time stone circle, where the stones had all fallen, was re-erected within the grounds of the community at Brithdir Mawr (*see also pages 165 and 166*). The author was not involved in this toil, but six years ago undertook a theodolite survey of the finished result. All but three of the stones fitted extremely well the 'Type I Egg' design discovered by Professor Thom, a rare surprise. Were these three stones to be placed back in their fallen positions and re-erected with their *other* ends upright, the design would correspond very closely to the geometry shown on the left of page six here. Which brings me to an important point for would-be 'restorers', professional or amateur. The original stone hole locations have been lost at Meini Gwyr, as have the original positions of recumbent stones at Brithdir. Without a half decent site plan these sites, even restored, are of far less use in the future evaluation of their astronomical and geometrical validity, and the site immediately becomes of no interest whatsoever to archaeologists, now or in the future.

The author has found what appear to be the remains of at least eight other stone circles within the boundaries of the Preselis, but these are all ruinous. However the locations of each stone has been recorded in case the world ever wakes up to the historical importance of these monuments.

This look at the sites ends with the two fine standing stones shown below. It is regretfully incomplete - but by omitting disappointing sites and those that lie on private land this guide remains usefully compact.

Two big standing stones, one free-range and the other behind bars. The left-hand stone is one of a pair at Cwm Garw, off the road from Mynachlog-ddu to Maenclochog. The largest stones found in the region, both the two Carn Garw stones lean such that a 'v' notch is formed. Looking through this notch, the local horizon is just visible, suggestive of a significant direction. The Lady Stone sits on the left-hand side of the Fishguard to Dinas Cross waiting for passers-by to doff their hats, according to a local tradition. Behind it can be seen the smallest flock of sheep in Pembrokeshire.

Waun Mawn
Waun Mawn pair
Ckydach stone
Outlier stone at Carreg y Gof
Preseli Megaliths
Three standing up & one lying down

Chapter Three

A First Glimpse of Otherworld

In the Celtic countries there is a strong tradition of saviour heroes, saints and other folk who in life have 'done good', then been spirited away after death to the Otherworld. Perhaps the best known story of is that of King Arthur who, following his mortal wounding at the battle of Baden Hill was taken to the Isle of Avalon, an Otherworld haven or Heaven, where his wounds were tended and from where, we are told, he will someday return to save Britain. Although the (once) Island of Glastonbury (Ynys Afalon) is traditionally associated in British folklore as Arthur's burial place, there is an equally strong tradition linking Arthur's final resting place as being either Bardsey Island (*shown below*) or Lundy Island in the Bristol Channel. These two island 'fortresses' off the coast of Wales were seen by the Celts as 'Isles of the Dead' and both of them, Bardsey and Lundy, can be seen from the Preseli hills.

Holy islands formed gateways to the Otherworld and the illustrious dead would be ferried there, 'to be buried with solemn rite amid the spirits of their

Bardsey Island from the East

forefathers'. Caer Sidi, often translated as 'the fortress of the faery folk', or of the wise or spiritually minded, is another example of the Otherworld kingdom. The Welsh bard Taliesin tells of its 'corners being washed by ocean's currents' - which tells us these places were clearly islands.

On a clear day, from the higher ground of the Preselis there are some fabulous views to be had. Once a traveller reaches five hundred feet (150m) above sea-level, the landscape offers perspectives which are quite often remarkable and certainly always memorable. On a clear day! When the fog or mizzle is down, a grey curtain falls and the horizon becomes confined to a mile or two, and sometimes only a few tens of feet. But on a clear day, Bardsey stands out like a dark pyramid rising from the sea horizon off the tip of the Lleyn peninsula. Light from Bardsey's lighthouse, although below the horizon, can be observed always left of the conical shape of Bardsey Mountain, which from here is seen 'end on'.

From the same period as the origin of the Arthurian stories, in the ecumenical tradition, there is reliable written and physical evidence that the mortal remains of Welsh heroes, holy men and saints within the Celtic Church were taken by boat from Mwnt, near Cardigan, to Bardsey, that tiny island located off the end of the Lleyn peninsula in North Wales. In many of these stories the dear departed are expected to make an eventual return back onto the mortal plain, but not always as saviours. There are many stories of folk who have accidentally stumbled into the faery realms and been taken in, often as lovers or, in the case of children, brought up by the faery folk. In most cases a yearning to return to the mundane world from whence they were once taken becomes irresistible despite dire warnings as to the consequences of so doing, and the classic climax of such stories is that they eventually succumb to this temptation only to recognise with shock that hundreds, perhaps thousands of years have elapsed since their departure. In some of the many variants of this tale the abductees crumble away to dust as soon as they touch the earth from whence they were once taken. We learn from these tales that in the Otherworld time passes at a vastly slower rate than on Earth, or even ceases.

The Otherworld tradition goes back far further than Celtic folklore. It derives from a prehistoric Polar tradition, based on the polar axis around which the whole earth rotates. It was once believed that this axis was the place from where human souls came into incarnation, and to where their souls would return when they shed their mortal coil. It is the tradition of the 'World Tree' or *axis mundi*, a most ancient tradition having much to do with the Great Bear, the circumpolar constellation used throughout known history to identify this axis, with or without a Pole Star currently taking residence there. The 'spiral castle' attributed to Caer Sidi and the concept of time cycles passing much more slowly in the Otherworld are often allegories of the daily ever-turning axis of the earth being compared with the precessional cycle of the Earth, which takes nearly 26,000 *years* to complete one similar cycle. Slowly but inexorably, the sunrise on a given date appears to move backwards against the Zodiac stars, one degree (nearly one day) every human lifetime, in comparison with taking a whole year to complete its revolution around the Zodiac, or a single day for the Earth itself to make a revolution around the sky, a phenomenon we all enjoy daily by experiencing the sun, moon and stars appearing to make a revolution above our heads!

My involvement with Bardsey and the reckoning of different ideas about time began slowly as such things tend to do in the Preselis. During a casual walk across Carningli common on a perfectly sunny windless day in late summer I became aware of how clear the distant landscape was. For the very first time I saw the whole of the Lleyn Peninsula in North Wales and in so doing, this enlarged my personal horizons. It was also possible to see the peaks of Cader Idris and Snowdon. The mountains along the Lleyn appeared as a string of dark islands, the curve of the Earth stealing from sight their lower regions and hiding the fact that their peaks are joined together and hence that these 'islands' are in reality mountains and hills with their roots joined together in the solid rock of North Wales. At the left hand end of this string of 'islands' there stands a final and quite differently shaped island, a real island this time, Bardsey, in Welsh *Ynys Enlli*.

This tiny island, often so difficult to get to by boat, kept on drawing my attention as I walked across the common from Bedd Morris to Carningli summit. I knew nothing then of its past nor even of its present. But looking at my maps on that pleasant afternoon while sat munching a sandwich on

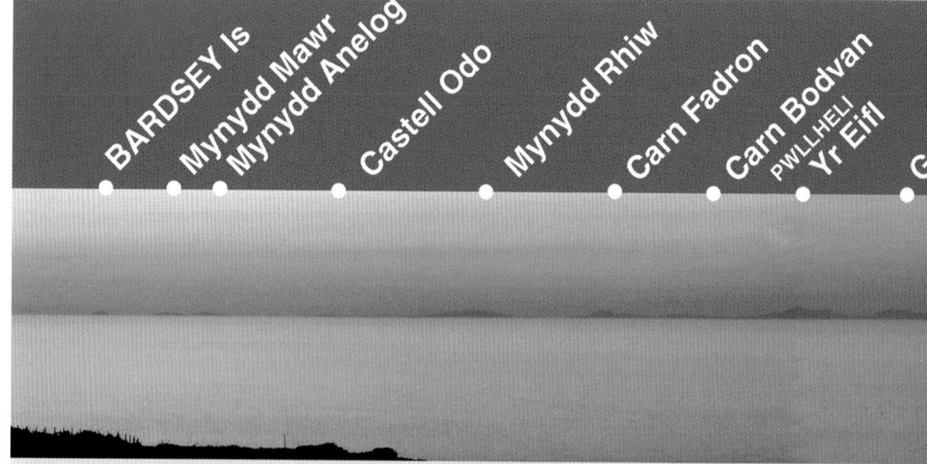

View northwards across Cardigan Bay from the coastal road

a rock at Carn Llwyd, I discovered that Bardsey Island fell almost directly north of Carningli. At nearly fifty miles range, Bardsey is not very often visible, but when it is, it provides a ready compass north-point to walkers in the Preseli hills. Eventually Bardsey's northness began to interest me again, as had its legends. I learned that, out of all proportion to its diminutive size, this tiny island has played an immense role in Welsh history. Twenty thousand saints or wise men are reputed to be buried there, and it is the *only* place amongst thousands where *both* Arthur and Merlin are reputed to lie buried. I made a visit with some friends, or perhaps it was a pilgrimage, to see if I could unravel any of the island's secrets.

On a clear night on Bardsey, looking south, it is possible to identify the red lights which festoon the modern TV mast at Crymych. On a clear day the entire Preseli profile can be identified from Garn Fawr to Carningli peak, Preseli top (Cwmcerwyn) and all along the ridge to Frenni Fawr (*photograph overleaf*). I asked myself an obvious question: *Where in the Preselis may the summit of Bardsey Mountain be observed precisely in the North?* Despite all my involvement with megalithic sites in the Preselis I had not once checked to see from which locations Bardsey Mountain appeared directly due north.

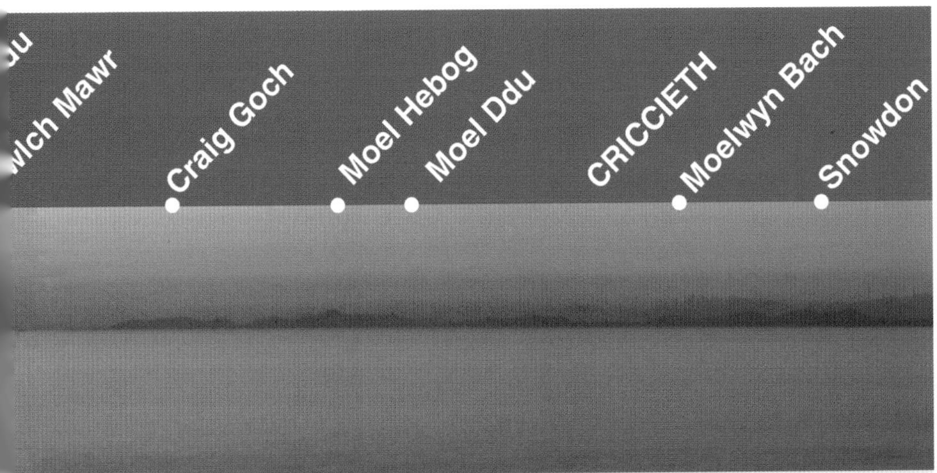

ech y Drybedd dolmen - midsummer evening, around 10:20pm

The north line to a visible Bardsey begins at Bwlch Pennant, about a mile from the crazy car park at Bwlch Gwynt described in the previous chapter. Walking eastwards towards the peak of Cwmcerwyn - Preseli Top - the highest point in the Preseli range, Bardsey is then nearly fifty-seven miles away. Tracing this line northwards I was pleasantly surprised to discover that the triangulation station ('trig point') on the top of the almost flat plateau of Carn Meibion Owen was sited directly on the precise North-South line to Bardsey, and *en route* to Bardsey this alignment then crosses the highest ground on the Moylgrove to Newport coastal road, some 607 feet above sea level. Here a second Trig point lies almost hidden half buried deep within a gorse-infested hedge where it too marks the line adjacent to a farmstead named, perhaps unsurprisngly...*Lleine*.

The Ordnance Survey map-makers had clearly discovered the 'Northern Line' to Bardsey before me, and made use of it in their survey of Wales. To a map maker, a 50-odd mile distant and pointed target like Bardsey Mountain would be impossible to resist. But the Ordnance Survey people had not been the first there - by about 5,000 years! People living in the Preselis many millenia before the Ordnance Survey came into existence had

The view south from Bardsey. Even at lower levels on the island it is possible to see the Preseli range, At night the red transmitter lights near Crymych are clearly visible.

discovered this target and employed it within their megalithic constructions. Five thousand years ago the people who built Pentre Ifan had also found the target irresistible - and it was duly recognised, honoured and incorporated into their landscape.

That our modern Ordnance Survey surveyors understood that Bardsey would make an excellent target to define a long North-South line traversing Cardigan Bay indicates how the mind of a surveyor works. Surveyors will always use natural features such as sharp peaks and prominent landmarks to establish reference points on the landscape and, as we will now discover, surveyors over five thousand years ago made use of Bardsey in similar fashion, leaving their handiwork on the landscape as a near perfect demonstration of their expertise as surveyors *and providing certain proof that they understood the importance of establishing True North as the first step in any process of surveying*. That they did this with such accuracy is remarkable, employing astonishing ingenuity at these two major sites. Once one understands that they did master such a task (and why) it instantly changes one's view both of what these people were thinking about, and their capabilities.

Less than half a mile to the east of a line connecting the two OS trig points lie two familiar megalithic sites, both of which command our attention in later chapters. Llech y Drybedd stands almost directly east of the trig point at Lleine, and if one was to climb onto the top of the huge capstone - which of course one mustn't - *it is possible to see Bardsey Island.* When the monument was covered in an earthen mound, as it is thought by many archaeologists to once have been, such an observation would be naturally made. The angle to Bardsey from this point is now very slightly in error, and falls a small amount short of truly North-South, at 359° 22', or 38 minutes of a degree west of True North. Directly south from Llech y Drybedd one can see Pentre Ifan, the defining monument of the Preselis. From the front of the capstone at Pentre Ifan, Llech y Drybedd lies at an azimuth of just 57 minutes west of True North.

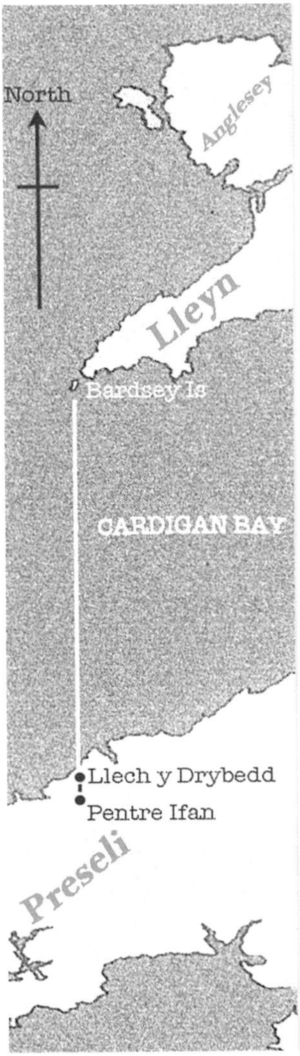

Llech y Drybedd thus acts as a northern foresight to Bardsey from Pentre Ifan - it stands directly in line with Bardsey and Pentre Ifan, on the very top of the ridge which prevents intervisibility between these two locations. Llech y Drybedd thereby connects an observer at Pentre Ifan with the orientation of Bardsey, perhaps as a sign-post to a sacred Otherworld island, and certainly to a credibly accurate North-South alignment (*illustrations right & overleaf*). In a later chapter the astronomy of Llech y Drybedd and Pentre Ifan are discussed at length and these sites seen as key players in an interplay between astronomical and geometrical wizardry.

It is hard not to see in the shape of the capstone of Llech y Drybedd a close match to the shape of Bardsey Island. Viewed from behind the monument, from the south - it resembles the shape of Bardsey Mountain to a remarkable degree. Of course we know nothing about whether

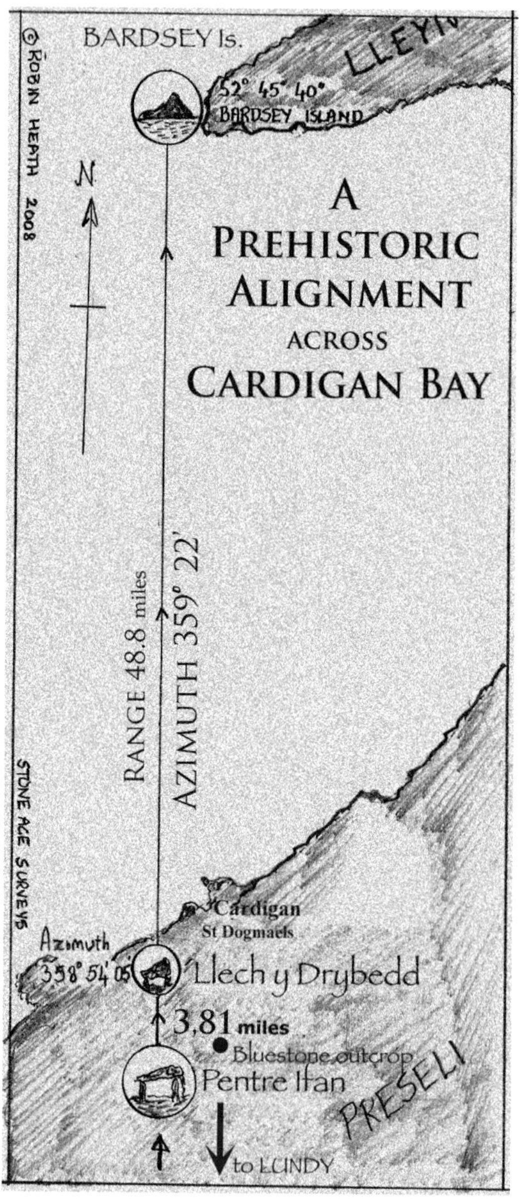

this was intentional or not. But a true *fact* has emerged: we now know that these two famous megalithic sites were sited to form a north-south alignment with Bardsey Island. Llech y Drybedd was certainly erected no earlier than 2500 BC, Pentre Ifan a millenium previously, making this perhaps the oldest evidence of applied surveying yet discovered anywhere in the world.

Bardsey had led me twenty years later to a doorway leading directly into the minds of people who lived in an Otherworld of sorts, a place from another time whose monuments have endured all time while we have not taken enough time to understand their intent, which until now has eluded us.

Bardsey is not the only island visible on a clear day from the Preselis. Looking south from Foel Eryr, Cwmcerwyn or any of the higher points on the southern side of the uplands it is possible to catch a glimpse of Lundy island, sitting in the Bristol Channel some 30 miles south of Tenby. Caldey Island, which has remained a monastic holy island since the earliest days of Christianity, lies a mile off the coast near Tenby, and stands directly in front of Lundy. At night the automatic lighthouses on both these Islands can be seen flashing one above the other from many vantage points high in the Preselis.

Lundy derives its name from the Scandinavian word for a Puffin, a reminder of the Viking incursions into this part of Britain during the centuries prior to the Norman ('northman') invasion proper. Lundy remained on the Welsh rolls long after the Normans and was entered thus in the Domesday book. In Welsh, Lundy Island was Ynys Elin, and the island retains its independence from the mainland in a way that remains one of the most interesting features of small islands. Unlike the Isle of Man, it has retained the vestiges of its own currency, made up of units called Puffins. It has always set its own licensing laws from the single public house on the island, The Marisco Tavern.

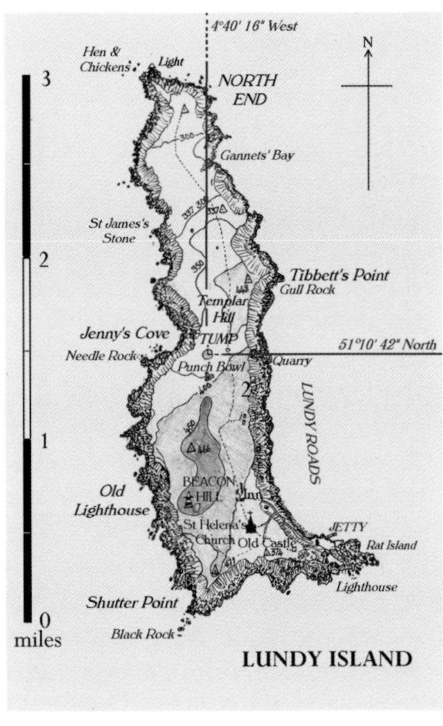

The older Celtic Christian church is dedicated to St Helen, guardian of the trackways, while the newer and incongruous church is dedicated to St Helena. Lundy has been variously owned by Vikings, smugglers and pirates, important familes and chivalric groups, being at some time owned by powerful Norman families like the Mariscos, the Knights Templar and, more recently by the Heaven family, an ownership which led to the construction of a Palladian manor and the island becoming referred to as *the Kingdom of Heaven*! It is truly one of most wonderful islands off the coast of Britain.

In modern times there has ceased to be a regular ferry service to Lundy from Wales, which has had the social effect of making the island even further away from Wales and nearer to Ilfracombe or Bideford in North Devon. Here, the daily trips of the SS Oldenburg ferry supplies, day trippers, and climbers, naturalists and sometimes parties of megalithomaniacs to enter this remote Otherworld, a flattish north-south plateau three miles long and a half-mile wide, raised aloft on a 500 foot near vertical stone skirting and incongruously placed in the midst of the Bristol Channel.

If one takes a line through the middle of Lundy's axis and projects that line northwards it will cut the Welsh coast after passing a little to the east of Caldey Island, just skimming Monkstone Point and passing up west of Amroth to Login and into the Preselis. During its passage through West Wales it passes within a quarter mile of the summit of Carn Wen, similarly the top ridge of Foel Drwrch, half a mile from the summit of Foel Drygarn, cutting the intriguing St Michael or Llanfihangel site now marked as 'Pile of Stones', where once the Golden Way, along the spine of the Preselis, came back down to the lower levels. It runs through many notable sites (*including St Dogmaels Abbey and Mwnt*) as it tracks northwards into North Wales, and southwards through Cornwall. The southerly extension has been amply covered within *The Secret Land* (Mythos Press, 2009), a collaboration with fellow researcher and Cornish historian Paul Broadhurst.

Two North-South Lines to Two Otherworld Islands

This second imaginary north-south line thus frames the eastern boundary of the Preselis while the Bardsey alignment frames the western side of the main ridge of the Preselis. Is something going on here? The two lines are separated by a little under seven minutes of longitude, a corridor less than five miles in width at this latitude and which encloses the central high ground of the Preselis. Right in the middle of this corridor one finds the outcrop quarries where the famous bluestones were obtained, for presently unclear reasons connected with Stonehenge.

In a later chapter a third polar axis will be discussed, again running through the landscape of West Wales.

We now know that the direction of north was an important concern for the megalith builders for them to have sited a number of their most impressive mounuments to align to the Pole. This is new and very significant information that has so far eluded the archaeologists. We also now know that their builders possessed the intellectual capacity to find true north together with the technology to implement this feat.

A visit to the high ground of the Preselis will, on a clear day, reveal both these islands. From Cwncerwyn, Bardsey is due north; from Carn Wen, Lundy is due south. Both are small specks on the horizon, needing binoculars to reveal any detail, yet they once assumed an important significance to a culture that appear to have attributed great importance to determining north and south on their landscape. The placement of Llech y Drybedd directly inline with Pentre Ifan and Bardsey Island provides the strongest evidence yet that precision surveying activities were being undertaken in prehistory - a line between two major monuments pointing to Bardsey is one thing, but an accurate north-south line is quite another!

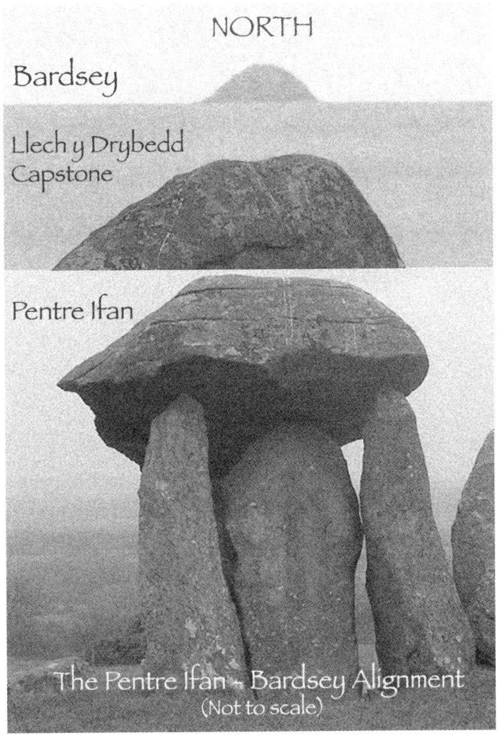

The Pentre Ifan - Bardsey Alignment
(Not to scale)

These 'Otherworld' islands stand either side of the most important question about our understanding of Stonehenge, and a big mystery: The bluestone site is located right there in the middle. *Might this be one reason why the bluestones assumed so much significance that they warranted the vast effort required to translocate them to Stonehenge?* It is a question to which we will return shortly.

You do not need to be an astronomer to appreciate a fine sunset, or a full moonrise, but if you want to know where and at what time the sun and moon will rise or set on a given day, the phase of the moon or when the next high tide or eclipse will occur, then it helps! Page 174 offers a start. The website www.skyandlandscape.com provides more details on how you can learn all these techniques.

Midsummer sunset at Llech y Drybedd, a monument located and designed to integrate with, and respond to, this annual event. All three photos have the sun on the sea horizon at the solstice, and then the design features really come alive for the visitor.

The most northerly full moonrise, a photosequence taken on 21st December 2006. This event only occurs every 230 full moons, and if you miss it..well, you'll just have to wait.

Chapter Four

Drawing down the Sun & Moon

In temperate regions, the axial tilt of the earth causes the climatic changes that have come to be known as the four seasons. Spring, summer, autumn and winter follow in an eternal round, with corresponding and remarkable changes to both skyscapes and landscapes. Because the skyscape is an essential component of the whole experience of landscape, anybody who enjoys being outdoors, or who paints or sketches, will well understand how important the light is to an appreciation of landscape. Each season brings a different experience of any landscape, and this coupled with the changing light conditions during different times of the day means that travelling through any landscape is never the same twice. These seasonal and daily changes are the result of the way the sun behaves in the sky above the landscape, and whether or not there are clear or cloudy conditions.

Observing the Sun

Except around midwinter and midsummer, each day finds the sun rising from a different place on the horizon, although if you walk the same patch regularly over a year or two it quickly becomes clear that, at the latitude of West Wales, both the sunrise and sunset are always contained within an arc of about eighty degrees equally spaced either side of true East (sunrises) and true West (sunsets). Around the latitude of the Preselis, at and around midwinter, the sun will rise in the south-eastern part of the sky, and set in the south-western part. It will be low in the sky even at noon, reaching only

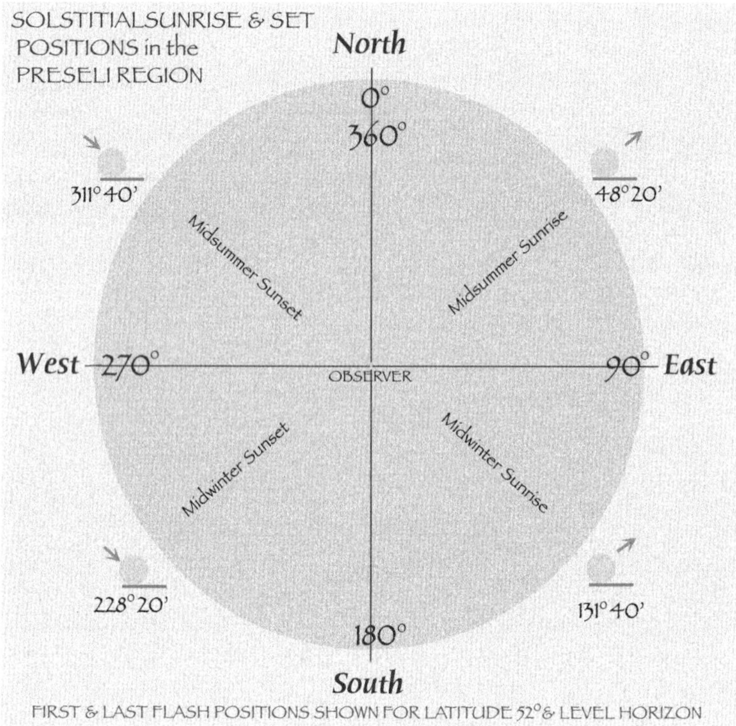

about 14.5 degrees elevation when it transits across the meridian, directly due South, at midday. The days will be short, sunrise occurring around eight in the morning and sunset around four in the afternoon.

At and around midsummer, the sun will rise in the north-eastern part of the sky, before five o'clock in the morning, and set in the north-western part of the sky after half-past nine in the evening. It will reach its highest ever elevation, again at local noon, reaching an elevation of about 62 degrees when it transits the South point. Around the longest day, it can be sunny for over seventeen hours and dusk is a long twilight period pushing the fading daylight northwards and well into the night period such that it never really becomes dark. The northern horizon remains at twilight throughout the short night.

These two extremes of the year are called the **solstices**, meaning that the sun's position of rise and set against the horizon appears to stop, dawn on dawn or evening on evening. At the summer solstice, anywhere in the world except in the polar regions, this stationary rising and setting position occurs on June 21st, while the midwinter solstice occurs on December 21st.

Roughly in-between these two station points in the year, day and night become, for just one single day, of equal length, at the **spring equinox**, on March 20th or 21st, and the **autumn equinox**, on September 22nd or 23rd. On just these two days in the year the sun rises directly East and sets directly West.

Equinox at 52 degrees north: sunrise 7:07 sunset 19:15. [Maximum (local noon) elevation 38 degrees]

Winter solstice: sunrise 8:25 sunset 16:10 [Max elevation 15 degrees]

Summer solstice: sunrise 5:00, sunset 21:43. [Max elevation 62 degrees]

These horizon positions are shown in the diagram opposite

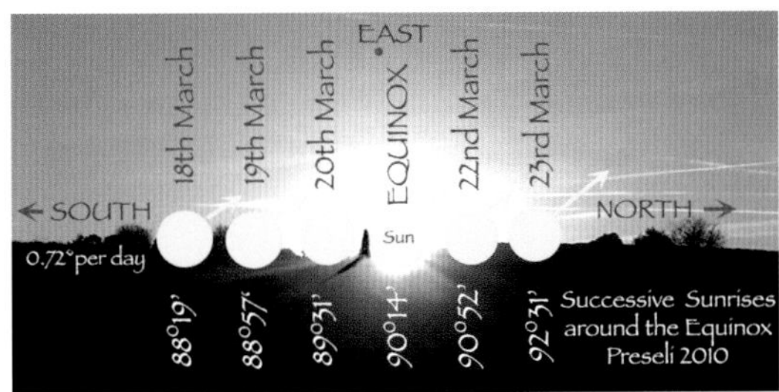

On the day of the spring or autumn equinox it would be hard to miss the sun rising (or setting) behind a prominent horizon marker. A day-tally of marks from one spring to the next would show 365 days as the year length, not 364 or 366 or any other number.

The length of the day changes fastest at the spring and autumn equinox. Within the fifteen days either side of the equinox the sun has moved along the horizon, both when rising and when setting, by about ten degrees, so that each day sees the sun rise and set by more than its own diameter, which is about half a degree. This daily change is so obvious that it is easily possible to determine accurately the length of the year, and this is what appears to have been going on within the megalithic culture. Just as we today require that our modern calendar must track as perfectly as possible the seasonal ebb and flow of the year, so too the neolithic culture, dependent on local seasonal hunting and agriculture would have been drawn to understand such things.

Our modern science has determined the length of the solar year, the time it takes for the Earth to orbit around the Sun, to within a minute fraction of a second of the 365.2422 day figure printed in almost any astronomy book. Using atomic clocks, computer technology and huge telescopes somehow convinces us that an accurate figure can only be acquired by cultures possessing the high trappings of technology, yet this is not actually true. There is strong evidence in the Preseli region that the neolithic astronomers knew how to construct monuments that would have enabled them to measure the length of the year to an accuracy within a few hours using only their eyes and long distance alignments.

The Preseli region is rich in prehistoric sites which display an astonishingly variety of astronomical functions. Most of the evidence presented in this chapter is original, the result of over twenty-five years observation and measurement in the landscape. This work began as an extension of a long interest in landscape walking. For many years the wilder areas of Britain provided joyful release from the madness of the modern world and placed me in contact with an infinite variety of textures, topologies and seasonal perspectives, together with a rich flora and fauna. Because the skyscape is an essential component of the whole experience of landscape, anybody who enjoys such things, or who paints or sketches, will instinctively recognise that the sites to be described here do indeed represent neolithic observatories for drawing down the motions of the sun and the moon onto the local landscape.

Neolithic Observatories

Prehistoric astronomy may have begun with the necessity of understanding the seasons as lengths of time, but this would have inevitably led to an understanding of the year as a length of days, a recurrent cycle. It appears that the curiosity of the prehistory astronomers then drove them to discover other cycles of time in the skies above their heads. Many prehistoric sites throughout the world are deliberately located such that a prominent visible horizon feature, natural or built, is oriented to key dates in the solar or lunar calendar. These sites, called backsights, mark significant rising and setting positions of the sun and moon against a distant horizon viewed from a second megalithic site, called a foresight. In the last century, the Astronomer

Royal, Sir Norman Lockyer and later Professor Alexander Thom found that some of these sites were remarkably precisely aligned to key sun and moon positions and this exposed a previously unexplored and certainly unexpected aspect of prehistoric life which found no easy place within the then current model of prehistory being peddled by archaeologists. As is often the case with discoveries that do not fit with the orthodox model, this new evidence was refuted and then vigorously ignored. For almost half a century the subject of archaeoastronomy has been stalled, waiting in the wings to reveal this astonishingly rich component into the overall picture we have of prehistoric life.

The present stance held by archaeologists, while inconvenient, may be effectively bypassed, by anyone prepared to make a little effort to assess the evidence, learn some basic astronomy and to retain an open mind. The use of GPS devices and modern computer technology such as Google Earth has greatly simplified the technical side of this subject and has made the astronomical assessment of sites possible to almost anyone who has an interest in the matter.

Within this chapter I have assumed nothing concerning the reader's knowledge of astronomy, and have assessed the Preseli observatories through the eyes and motives of a neolithic astronomer. However, for those who wish to acquire more of the technical details of each survey, there are illustrated survey reports on my website www.skyandlandscape.com. I have also embedded a basic primer in the subject, and the required astronomical formulae, to assist the reader.

Why has archaeoastronomy, a word guaranteed to sound complicated and to put off many people otherwise interested in ancient astronomy, enshrouded itself with the techniques and terms of modern astronomy when most if not all of these terms were unknown to the builders of the monuments? It's a good question, because such an approach is a projection of the modern world back into the past. However, and most unfortunately, it is a necessary projection because of one unavoidable physical fact: since the Neolithic period the tilt of the earth's axis has steadily reduced so that the positions of sun and moon rises and sets have changed by nearly a degree.

To discover where the luminaries rose and set at the time when the sites were built - to see the site operating as the builders would have done - requires knowledge of the mathematical and astronomical formulae.

The neolithic builders had no need for theodolites, astronomical almanacs, ephemerides and degree level maths. Unencumbered by all the modern paraphernalia required by archaeoastronomy, their task was simply to define a straight line between their observing location and some marker on a distant horizon that marked sunrise or sunset on the longest or shortest day of the year. They just aligned their monuments to the spot on the horizon where the sun 'stopped' at midwinter or midsummer. Every year they had another chance to improve on the accuracy until, once they were satisfied, they could erect a suitable monument as the backsight and another as the foresight.

From Moylgrove to Fishguard there are a varied number of monuments which record the position of the summer solstice sunset. It is to these monuments, already described in the previous chapter, that we now investigate as astronomical solar observatories. Each detects midsummer sunset yet each is adapted to perform this role in a way that is beautifully tailored to match the location.

Llech y Drybedd - Midsummer Alignment

A theodolite survey of the monument enabled the position of midsummer sunset from the site to be calculated for 2800 BC, the archaeologically reckoned date of construction. The axis of symmetry of Llech y Drybedd is aligned to this midsummer sunset, the way it does this and the accuracy of the alignment is astonishing.

The foresight is an exceptional 91 miles distant. Calculations show that in 2800 BC the sun set into the peak of Lugnaquilla in the Wicklow mountains of Ireland. The casual visitor to Llech y Drybedd is unlikely to see the Wicklow range way across the Irish Sea, but may be assured that on clear days it becomes visible as the 'island' mentioned in chapter one. Standing at the front of the monument, the alignment runs just to the left of the only tree in the banked field boundary some 100 yards from the monument. Even when the peak is not visible, there will often be cumulus clouds visible over the Wicklow range which mark its position. Some foresight, and what a feat of human endeavour to engineer the monument this way!

Llech y Drybedd - Midsummer solstice sunset, 1994

Even on midsummer eves where the Wicklow range is invisible, and for about a week either side of the solstice, the sunset here is utterly spectacular and the experience unforgettable. From behind the monument, the sun flashes in turn through the two triangular gaps formed between the rear two upright stones and the front one (*see right*). As the sun sets, the flat front of the huge capstone, which faces the midsummer sunset position, glows orange. Now look behind the monument where the Preseli range has taken on an orange hue, after sunset it darkens as the monument becomes increasingly grey and silhouetted against the fading of the light. This is a good time to reasonably adapt Henry James's description of Stonehenge, which sums up what people sometimes feel at ancient stones

Above: A photographic sequence of the midsummer sun setting into the Wicklow hills from Llech y Drybedd, in 1995, around 9:38 pm. The flat horizon is seen to be interrupted by the slopes of a mountain range in Ireland, some 91 miles distant.

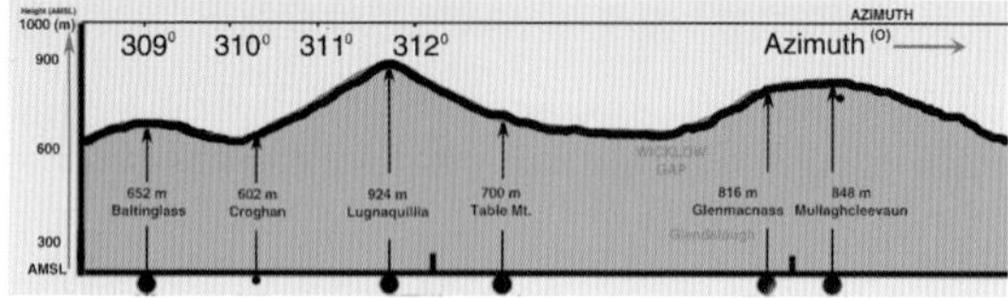

Above: Graphic of the midsummer sunset into the Wicklow mountains, based on the photograph sequence on the previous page. Below: An horizon profile shows the correspondences between the astronomy and the Wicklow mountains.

'There is something (at Llech y Drybedd) almost reassuring; and if you are disposed to feel that life is rather a superficial matter, and that we soon get to the bottom of things, the immemorial grey pillars may serve to remind you of the enormous backdrop of Time.'

Llech y Drybedd - A Midwinter Detector

During the midwinter solstice at Llech y Drybedd, the sunset lights up the inside of the front 'immemorial grey pillar' *(photograph opposite, left)*. It is the only time of year when this glancing ray can ever enter the chamber, as the sun sets into Mynydd Melyn. This orientation not as impressive as the midsummer alignment, but if intentional, it shows remarkable ingenuity of design. Many monuments, like Newgrange in Ireland, are aligned to midwinter sunrise or set, a function thought by anthropologists to symbolise the "death' of the sun, at its lowest point within the yearly cycle, to thereafter be reborn and rise again towards the following midsummer.

By investigating the astronomy of the sun at Llech y Drybedd we have greatly enlarged our knowledge of the monument. This makes clear that the location was very carefully and cleverly chosen, for additionally it provides the north

MIDWINTER SUNSET AT LLECH Y DRYBEDD

point from Pentre Ifan *en route* to Bardsey Island. To achieve these two objectives in one place, the builders were limited to a small strip of land on the coastal ridge above Moylgrove.

CarregCoetanArthur-Midsummer Alignment

Less than four miles further down the road to Newport, Coetan Arthur repeats the same function. The monuments' axis of symmetry is also aligned to midsummer sunset in or around 2800 BC, and the sun would have shone through the 'v' notch between the two back uprights, just as it does through the two triangles at Llech y Drybedd (*see photograph on page 45*). The solar astronomy of Coetan Arthur is more difficult to appreciate because the hedge in front of the monument obscures the view, as also do the wooded fields along the alignment. In winter, when there are no leaves, a theodolite reveals that the midsummer alignment would have passed by the large banked 'settlement' adjacent to the modern tennis courts.

Two dolmens both aligned in the same direction and doing much the same thing, and not a word about any of these things in the history books. Perhaps now this can change - perhaps this is a history book of the future!

Carreg Y Gof - Midsummer Alignment

This site offers an important modification that seems to have been applied to many sites, which were adapted as the extreme solstitial sunsets changed its position over the centuries with the reducing axial tilt of the earth.

There is a clue in the later site as to where to look. The right hand stone of the most northerly mini-dolmen mirrors perfectly the shape of Needle Rock (*see below*), and this seems unlikely to be accidental, and connects us in a most human way to the intentions of the builders of these 'stones of remembrance' (*Carreg Atgof*) which we had..er,..forgotten.

Copy-cat stones of. Needle Rock & Carreg y Gof. A message - look here for sunset?

The midsummer sunset from this location skims down the steep cliffs of Dinas Head and sets into the sea horizon (*photo opposite*). A very large cup-marked outlier stone (*page 64*), some 300 feet from the main site at Carreg y Gof was once, in the Neolithic, aligned to the midsummer sunset. This took place into the sea, directly above Needle Rock, which acted as a foresight. This arrangement offered a precision indicator of the midsummer solstice in neolithic times. Today the sun sets to the left of the rock, a spectacular place to watch solstice sunset.

The radial collection of ruinous mini-dolmens is built to the right of the stone looking to Needle rock, and would have acted as a similar backsight *at a much later date*, during the Bronze Age. This agrees with the dating for this monument offered from traditional archaeological evidence, confirmed independently from the astronomy of the location.

This alignment also connects back into the hinterland of Carningli common. Here is one very good place to watch the sun set around the week either side of the summer solstice, from Carn Llwyd or Carn Briw. Indeed, from here I watched the sun go down over Dinas Head many years before I found the solstice alignment from Carreg y Gof. It takes time to cover the territory.

All three of the coastal dolmens within the 'Newport Group' that have survived in reasonable condition reveal one major design feature - they were a backsight from where the midsummer sunset could be observed. To perform this task, *natural* landscape features were employed as a foresight, although there was once a large monolith in front of Llech y Drybedd 'towards the sea' perhaps employed when visibility across the Irish Sea was obscured, which commonly happens. Implied in this is that the actual *location* of the monuments was chosen in order to fulfil their astronomical roles.

Below From the cup-marked stone, the sun's disc would have touched the sea horizon directly over Needle Rock around 3500 BC. From the centre of Carreg y Gof, the same alignment would have been seen around 2000 BC. An archaeoastronomer concludes that the stone was there long before the dolmen.

The next site is rather different in that it provides two built sites and one natural site along the solar alignment. In addition, and most importantly in showing the intended purpose of the observatory, the backsight points to the foresight. And this next site is all about the *midwinter* sunset.

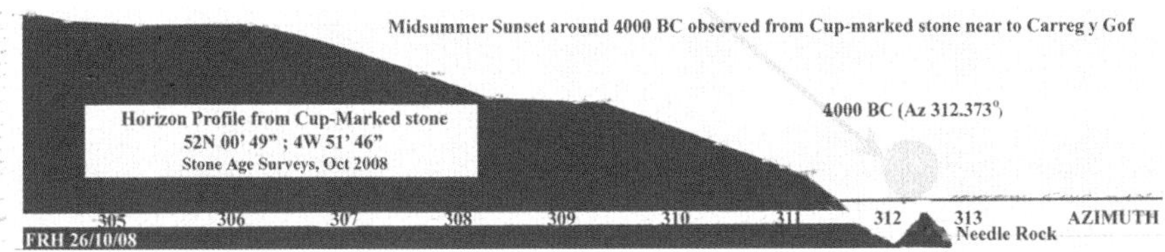

Pentre Ifan - Midwinter Alignment

Midwinter is often a difficult time on the higher ground of the Preselis, and there is not much evidence that it was significantly easier for the people that lived here five or six millenia ago. When days are cold and there is a biting north-westerly wind, one can imagine that enthusiasm for astronomical observation might have waned. The midwinter alignment at Pentre Ifan offers something of a compromise - the site isn't on a peak and there is some shelter from the icy winds provided by the parabolic forecourt to the south of the monument. From here, in 3500 BC, the sun would have been seen to slide down the right hand edge of the extreme left hand outcrop that forms Carn Meibion Owen. This outcrop marked the most southerly sunset of the year - midwinter - after which the sun would set along the ridge, a little more to the north each day.

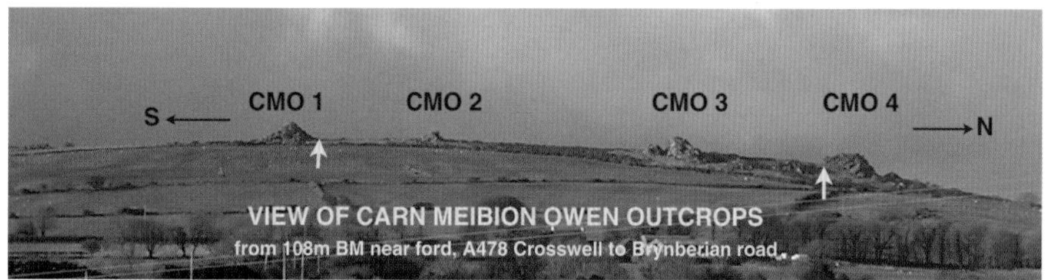

VIEW OF CARN MEIBION OWEN OUTCROPS
from 108m BM near ford, A478 Crosswell to Brynberian road

This alignment is further confirmed by the presence of a remarkably large stone found in the field once called Corlan Samson, (St Samson's fold) a few hundred feet below Pentre Ifan. This megalith has some remarkably helpful properties. Firstly, it is enormous and has two huge circular holes about a foot deep gouged out of one side, like the headlamp sockets on a scrap car. Secondly, it is also recumbent, and inspection reveals that it is comprised of two separate megaliths, the smaller of which possesses a level flat platform, and a long flat side edge which actually points to Pentre Ifan!

These features (*shown opposite left and on page 39*) are like gold to an archaeoastronomer, because they are a message from prehistoric times saying 'We were here!' and 'Look towards Pentre Ifan!' Which I duly did, with

Above left: The flat edge and level platform of the smaller stone at Maen Corlan Samson which points to Pentre Ifan and the right-hand edge of the first Carn Meibion Owen outcrop. In 3500 BC, the sun would have set at midwinter as shown in the right-hand photograph [azimuth 219°, elevation 4.7°]

theodolite, after being shown the stone by its 'discoverer', local nurseryman, Mr Suleyman Mowatt, a time served megalithomaniac of many years.

From the aligned stone, the midwinter sunset alignment is repeated, with the top of Pentre Ifan capstone now marking the alignment *en route* to the same foresight slope of the extreme left-hand outcrop of Carn Mebion Owen.

On a warmer day, I trundled my kit up to the outcrop above Pentre Ifan and confirmed the angles looking back from the foresight to both Pentre Ifan and Maen Corlan Samson (as I named this remarkable megalith which gets no mention in any of the literature about the Pentre Ifan site). Once the theodolite had been levelled and the readings taken I casually lifted up the eyepiece above Pentre Ifan to see if there were any more notable features along the alignment to the north-east. I suddenly found myself spying on a group of tourists entering the front door of the main roundhouse at Castell Henllys! Allegedly an Iron Age site, this surprise view suggested it was located *acknowledging* this midwinter alignment. Either continuity of function is suggested or the present site was built on a much older Neolithic site that no-one seems keen to talk about because it doesn't fit into the current model of prehistory. A strange thing, archaeoastronomy, sometimes it exposes large cracks in an otherwise cosy model of the past.

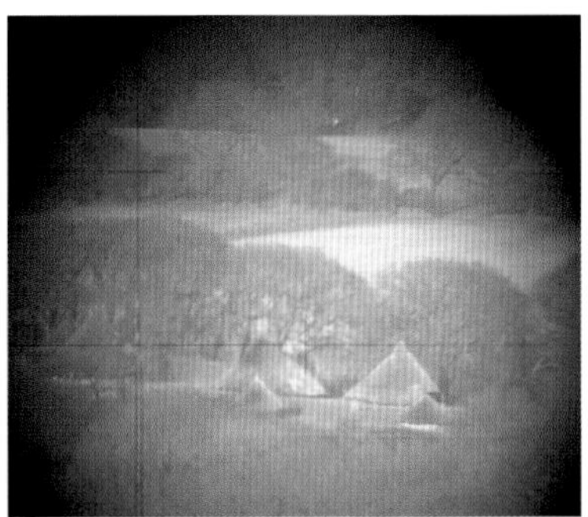

Looking from the foresight on Carn Meibion Owen (left) down the midwinter sunset alignment to Pentre Ifan, Maen Corlan Samson (adjacent to the tree behind Pentre Ifan) and...surprise, surprise, Castell Henllys. Extended further the alignment terminates on Cader Idris, marking the most northerly moonrise every 18.6 years.

Having found another important site on this alignment, I lifted the eye piece even higher. It broke the horizon at the grain silos near the five-way 'crossroads', just off the A487 at Croft. Immediately beyond this, the snow capped ridge of the sacred mountain of Cader Idris filled the eyepiece. At 61 miles range, this unexpected visual end to a local alignment that included four significant local sites was greatly of interest, because, from its end at Carn Meibion Owen, the most northerly moonrise in the lunar cycle of 18.6 years would have been seen rising out of Cader Idris. More on this later when we consider moon alignments.

One other site that is worth the early morning midsummer trek in the dawn twilight along the Drover's Way is Bedd Arthur. You will need to be there soon after 4:30 am, where in the absence of clouds, the sun will rise gloriously to the left of Foel Drygarn, at 4:38 am. In the absence of a marked foresight, this is not a precision alignment, only the axis of symmetry suggests where on the horizon one should look, a distant hilltop *en route* to Bettws Evan, Brynarthen, Glanarthen, Llanarth and Aberarth. All these 'Arth' places are significant indicators of ancient surveying having taken place, and will be explained in chapter seven.

If these few sites show that the extreme northern and southern rises and sets of the sun were being keenly monitored, what then of the equinoxes?

It is to these that we now turn, and the problems that neolithic astronomers faced when trying to establish the length of the year in order to understand the rhythms and cycles of the planet they found themselves on.

Equinoctial Alignments

The solstitial alignments informed prehistoric people when the summer and winter halves of the year had peaked. Paradoxically, when the sun was still against the horizon dusk on dusk or dawn on dawn, then the year moved on. If they had been able to tally the numbers of days between the two solstices, they would have discovered that about an equal number of days formed each half of the year, and that the length of the year was always the same number of tally marks, perhaps expressed as lengths - of notches, pebbles or of knots in a long rope. To find the midway between the two extreme positions of the sun, they had two choices. Either they could take a tally rope marked out in days from winter to summer solstice and fold it in half. In effect the day-marks indicated the equinox, or they could compare the two angles that indicated where the sun rose or set at summer and winter, and divide the angle into two and await the time in the year when the sun next rose or set at this angle.

Neither of these two choices employed processes that were beyond prehistoric builders. Their geometrical prowess is to be found scattered throughout northwestern Europe, using Pythagorean triangles, right angles, division of angles and angles defined with reference to True North. And while we may never know the chronology of how they came to know the accurate lengths of the solar year or lunar month, we do know that it was known, because it is reflected in the monuments themselves, here in West Wales. Here, there are tally marks deeply cut into granite, solstice alignments of various imaginative forms and geometries that demonstrate that these people knew what they were doing. It remains to demonstrate that they were familiar with the concept of 'equinox', and the best way to show that this is true is by identifying equinoctial sights.

Alignments to the equinoctal sunrises and sets must always run closely to an east-west axis. A monument or stone row closely aligned east-west will mark the rising and setting of the sun on the two days in the year when the day and night are of equal length - spring and autumn equinox. There is a good example in Preseli, at Russia, and it has already been mentioned on page 56. Like many monuments this one has survived because it has been pressed into service as very sturdy gateposts and the stones from which it was constructed were considered too large and too heavy to be worth moving. We will shortly return to this site, after investigating what I believe to be an earlier site that began this calendrical work. I believe, with some good reason, that this site was the culmination of astronomical observations undertaken at a nearby site where a near-equinoctial alignment provided by natural features impelled the neolithic society living on the Preseli hills to take 'a huge step for mankind' in their understanding of cosmic cycles, to wit, the solar calendar. The physical remnants of this alignment speak eloquently of its function, while the local folklore and history of the region confirms its importance and continuity into medieval times.

The St Davids Alignment

In the twelfth century, Bishop Bernard managed to persuade Pope Calixtus that two visits to St Davids would secure the same blessings for pilgrims as one to Rome would and thenceforth, from that time on, a well-trodden 'Pilgrim's Path' resounded to the tired feet of the devout as they plodded their way from wherever to the furthest western corner of West Wales.

Sections of this path can be found today, together with town names that resonate to Templar, Masonic and Catholic practices - Croes Goch (Red Cross), Square and Compass and Mesur y Dorth (Measure of Bread). But there are also inconvenient megalithic sites placed all along the same path, virtually a straight line from Carningli (Mountain of Angels) to St David's Head, adjacent to the Cathedral and the once walled and gated town named after Wales' patron saint. What are all these megaliths doing here, along a twenty mile pilgrim's path? Certainly, nothing that the Church wanted to know anything about!

One answer as to why all those pre-Christian sites crop up along the entire route may be the presence of two distinctive peaks that rise up out of the flat landscape as one reaches St Davids - Penberi and Carn Llidi. From Carningli these appear as a grail or cup above the distant sea horizon. The sun sets into this cup each and every February 18th. On the days either side it misses, and the cup thus provides a perfect foresight to determine with the naked eye that the length of the seasonal or solar year is 365 days and not 364 or 366 days. Here is what you see.

The St Davids Alignment

February the 18th is not the date of the spring equinox, but it falls near enough such that the daily change in the position of sunset is more than the solar disc's diameter. To see the sun set into the cup would impel anyone to keep their eyes on sunsets thereafter. Natural human curiosity being what it is, we may be assured that prehistoric people noticed this one-day wonder in their midst. A few year's observation from Carningli or Mynydd Melyn and something else would reveal itself to the observers. So perfect is this natural site that it is easily possible, year on year, to also observe that there is a four year repeated cycle of positions for the final flash of the sun as it slides into the cup. All a megalithic sunwatcher needed to do was to scratch or tally the number of days between successive sets into that cup each spring (or autumn, for the set occurs twice a year) in order to discover that three years of 365 days counts are followed by a fourth year when 366 days are tallied, and the sunset returns to its original position. Thus in four years one tallies 1461 marks or notches, whence the year length can be found. Fold a marked rope in four and 'read' 365 and a quarter. It could have been that simple.

Feb 18th 2002
17:40:33 hrs
Last Flash
Last Flash 252.34 degrees

Weather prevented observation Feb 18th 2003

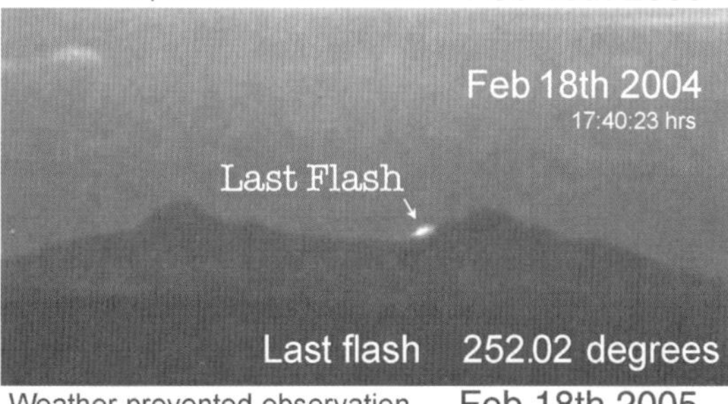

Weather prevented observation Feb 18th 2005

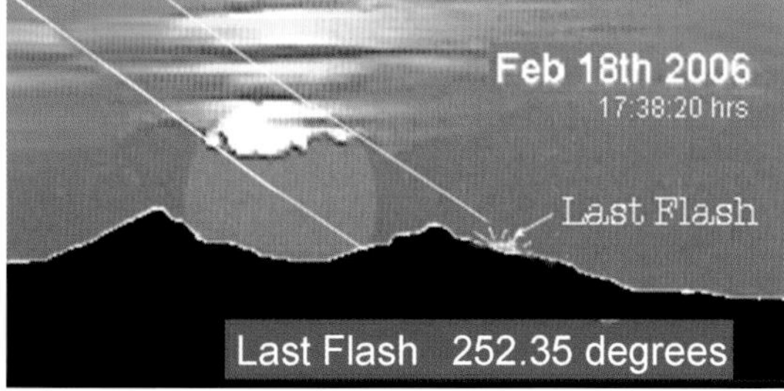

If this technique was applied, then the pre-historic astronomers would know the length of the year to within 11 minutes, a figure as accurate as our modern calendar, also of 365.25 days in length.

This is supported by the large number of megalithic sites spaced out along the alignment from Carn Ingli to the 'grail' or cup. This observatory would have assumed much importance in the community and provided it with a useful and accurate calendar.

There are big cairns, standing stones, tumuli earth-works, and ancient crossroads, even a sub-stantial dolmen at its termination, cupmarks on stones, aligned roads, trackways and footpaths and even the Welsh names of mountains support the social importance of this alignment. To verify this all you will need is an OS map and a long ruler.

From Carningli peak the alignment passes through Carn Briw, Bedd Morus standing stone, a cairn, an enclosure and hut circle on the southern side of Mynydd Melyn peak, a curious 'quarry' of large stones that provides the ideal viewing spot along the alignment, Llanychaer ford, Jordanstown crossroads, Llangloffan crossroads, Mathry centre, The burial chamber at Trewallter Farm, Square and Compass, Mesur y Dorth, Croes Goch, and between Penberi and Carn Llidi peaks and terminating at Coetan Arthur, an earthfast dolmen on St David's Head. In addition, the map will show places where the old trackways align with the alignment or run closely parallel to it. There are also various standing stones no longer shown on modern maps.

Ten centuries ago, all those hospitallers, priests and pilgrims were flocking to St Davids and they walked these pathways. But something was different then. In their time, the Roman 'Julian' calendar was no longer synchronised to the seasons and was running about eleven days ahead of the real seasonal date. In their time, real time February 18th was March 1st on their calendars - St David's day. A correction was eventually made - a reform of the calendar, in 1752, and the correction needed was to add eleven days. The alignment (to St Davids) is now seen to be directly linked with St David's day - the most important day in the Welsh calendar - named after Wales' patron saint, who we are told - by someone living during the reign of the old calendar - died (he set?) on March 1st, since rebranded to February 18th.

Within a mile of the alignment, there remains a living tradition centred around Pontfaen in the Gwaun Valley, called the Hen Galen (old calendar), where January 11th is still held to be the date of the New Year, following the pre-Gregorian calendar. Locally, it's a big deal, centering near a pub I love to visit, Bessie's Dyffryn Arms public house. The new calendar appears never to have been entirely integrated in these remote parts.

Finally, there are lots - I am tempted to say scores - of tally marks at the base of a huge granite outcrop called Carn Enoch, less than a mile from the alignment. The evidence stacks up to support the reality that some kind of prehistoric counting was established here, and that the 'twin peaks' were indeed used to establish an accurate calendar in prehistory. It is not unreasonable to assume megalithic cultures could arrange a simple counting process. Tally marks of days could be linearly represented along a rock, rope or stick as lengths of time. No mathematics are then required, simply day counting using a similar distance between each day. Time becomes length - *lengths of time*. Later, in chapter six we will look at traditional units of length and discover that astronomical ratios exist between them.

Carn Enoch

No one from the Church seems at all interested in any of this and the archaeologists don't want to pursue it either, the Church because the sites on 'their' pilgrimage route stem from pre-Christian pagan practices which were routinely destroyed wherever they were encountered, and the archaeologists because they avoid stone age astronomy like a medieval plague. Meanwhile there's a calendar on the Preselis that still works and which can 'fix' the year length to 11 minutes accuracy.

If one imagines that stone age astronomy evolved, then the practitioners of that art would gradually accrue a collection of factual knowledge about the astronomy of the sun, moon and stars. The angles for a midsummer sunset or midwinter sunrise would all be similar angles. The idea of counting days would naturally lead to the discovery that the February 18th alignment was not placed equally in days between the two solstices. It is 59 days or two lunar months from the winter solstice and 123 days, one third of the year, from the summer solstice. Thirty-two days would need to be added to the St Davids day date in order to find the middle ground - *the equinox*. The solar year is then marked into quarters of 91 days, which would then invite the curious to sub-divide again to eighths, each of about 45 days, perhaps even sixteenths, an oxymoronic 'solar month', perhaps better defined as a 'sunth' of 22 or 23 days. Fifty years ago, one man discovered evidence that this was indeed done, this design of calendar construction does indeed seem to have existed in prehistoric Britain. Most of the evidence we have for it comes from the work of Alexander Thom, who analysed hundreds of solar alignments throughout Britain and compared them on a histogram chart (*below*). The markers progressively bunch up near the solstices when the sun moves less per day along the horizon as it rises or sets, exactly as expected from the astronomy. Thom's histogram hit all the eighths and several of the sixteenths, leading him to suggest that a Stone-Age calendar was a reality, with 'months' of 22, 23 and 24 days in length, which when added up came to to 365 days.

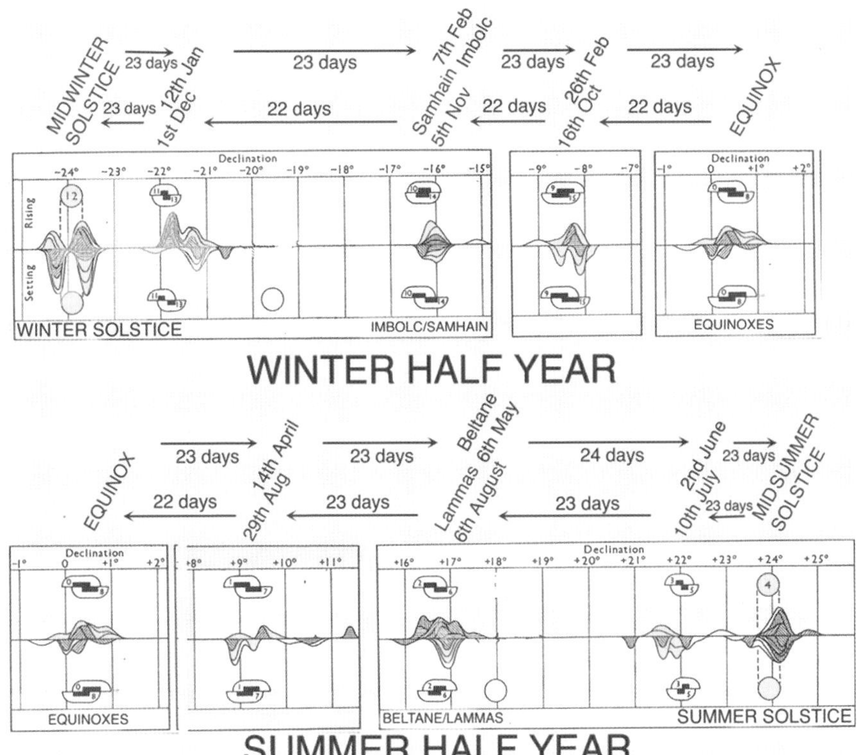

Prof Thom's evidence for a prehistoric 16 month calendar, based on over 100 alignments. The histogram shows clearly how these alignment 'bunch up' around the required dates of repeatedly dividing the year length by two, or folding a marked rope.

There is interesting additional confirmation that Thom was onto the truth of the matter. The equinox is today defined as the time in the year when the declination of the sun is zero. This is a definition only possible through knowledge of modern astronomical methodology, and would have been incomprehensible to a neolithic astronomer. *Their* equinox was defined by dividing the time between two solstices or the angle between two solstitial alignments in two. This determines a point in the year when the declination is not quite zero. Thom was able to measure this difference at site after site as being about plus half a degree - the calculated amount. Our culture has still to recognise the astonishing implications of this hard evidence for a prehistoric solar calendar, running throughout the British Isles.

The Russia Stones - Equinox Alignment

Three ostentatious bluestone gate posts are all that remain upright from what once appears to have been a well defined site for observing the setting sun at the equinoxes. It has to be considered most unfeasible that local farmers just happened to place their field boundaries and then their gates such that the arrangement is very accurately arranged in an east-west line, perfectly set up against the western horizon to record the day of the equinox and on a level site also with a view to the St Davids alignment foresight mountains! The modern road makes a detour to run along the alignment, indicative that there may have been a trackway there that was easily adapted to take the tarmac of modern times. And finally there is the size of the stones, they are whoppers!

The arrangement is shown on photographs on page 54, but the visitor needs to go and see this site, which is a mile or so from the pull-in on the left-hand side of the Dinas to Pontfaen road, about 200 yards from a cattle grid (*grid gwarthog* in Welsh) where the twin peaks of the St Davids alignment may be best viewed. On February 18th it is often good to have a vehicle nearby.

On the day of either spring or autumn equinox the sun sets in the gap between the two stones at the western end when viewed from behind the eastern stone, some 170 yards away. The four-year cycle of set positions can also be observed. To do this, you will need permission from the local farmer, contactable by asking the 'star' landlady Bessie at the Dyffryn Arms public house, just half a mile further down the hill in the Gwaun Valley. The photograph shows how the site records the equinoctial sunset, the cross-wires on the theodolite are set to 269° 4', the azimuth angle from the top of stone one to that of stone two in the arrangement. The disc of the sun is drawn to scale. In the roadside bank can be seen other very large monoliths that now lie recumbent and mute but perhaps were once part of this equinoctial observatory.

The Lunar Observatories

This is not the book to go into detail about the complex motions of the moon. All the reader needs to know here is that the moon covers all the rise and set positions that the sun occupies during the year, but completes this in only 27.32 days - one sidereal lunar month. In addition, these monthly extreme rises and set 'breathes' in and out, over an 18.61 year cycle, extending the two extreme rise and set positions each month 'outboard' of the solstitial sun for 9.3 years, and for a similar period when the monthly extreme rise and sets fall 'inboard' of the solstitial sun positions. The absolute extreme positions correspond to the major and minor standstills of the moon, which fall just under ten degrees either side of the four solstitial sun positions (*see overleaf*). There are thus eight positions on the horizon that correspond to these extreme lunar rises and sets, many of which can be found at sites in the Preseli region, as they can elsewhere.

The moon changes its rise and set positions much more quickly from day to day than does the sun, so anyone wanting to see the extreme set positions

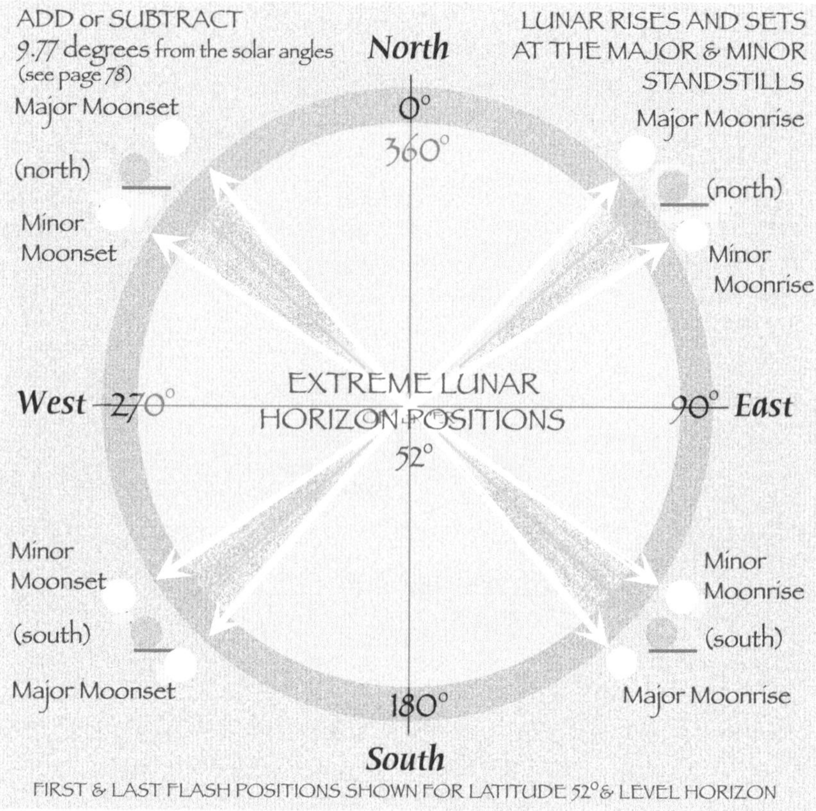

from a site (which can occur at any phase of the moon) will need to look up in tables or via the internet just when the monthly maximum and minimum declination occurs, and whether this occurs around moonrise or set. Only the keen win! However, for the less diligent moonwatcher, knowing where and when a moon rise or set will take place provides scope for experiencing some breath-taking moments at sites, and great photographs. For example, when full, the moon rises around the time of sunset and directly opposite the sun. While watching a really fabulous sunset near to the day of the full moon, there's often a second treat going on right behind you.

Parc y Meirw - Lunar Observatory

If the name doesn't put you off this splendid site - it means 'Field of the Dead' after a medieval battle that reputedly took place there - then the parking will. Parc y Meirw is now part of a banked Pembrokeshire field boundary and a narrow road runs alongside it (*see photograph on page 54*).

The site became identified as a lunar observatory when Alexander Thom and his son came down from Scotland for a few days surveying here in 1964. Marked on the map as a 'stone row', Thom was drawn like a magnet to survey the site. A theodolite survey revealed that the stone row was aligned to the extreme minor moonset in the north, which from the location is at an azimuth angle of 301.4 degrees. In addition, upon his return home, Thom discovered that the distant foresight was Mount Leinster in Ireland, some 93 miles away. In 1994 I was able to see this 'island' on the sea horizon beyond Fishguard, from the site, alas not with the moon at standstill.

Why would anyone need to accurately record the minor standstill moonset in the north, then or now? It turns out that if you wish to be able to understand and even predict when eclipses are likely to occur, then only at the standstill periods, every 9.3 years can this be achieved using an observatory like Parc y Meirw and naked eye astronomical observation. The moon has an up and down wobble of about 0.15 degrees during a cycle of 173.3 days, and eclipses can only occur when it is at the top of this cycle. The extreme standstill rise or set becomes a super-standstill at this time, altering where the moon rises or sets by a detectable amount.

The stones that make up the present row are huge, and there are others recumbent in the bank which can easily be seen from the road side. There is parking after a fashion up the ramp that leads to the gated entrance to the 'Field of the Dead'. You will need permission if you want to enter this field, from the farmer at Trellwyn farm, on whose land stand other large stones which may once have been part of the lunar alignment.

The modern maps just identify this site as 'standing stones', the earlier maps say 'stone row'.

Llech y Drybedd - Lunar Observatory

An excellent example of a precision lunar observatory can be found around Llech y Drybedd. Earlier this dolmen's role as the backsight of a precision solar observatory was discussed. A short distance foresight was probably provided by the now missing large upright stone 'towards the sea' reported to archaeologist Richard Fenton in the 18th century, but the ultimate foresight was the peak of Lugnaquilla in County Wicklow, in Ireland.

As a lunar observatory, Llech y Drybedd takes the role of providing the foresight, and the backsite is a level 'henge' monument, y Gaer, found within 1.5 miles of Llech y Drybedd. Between this site and the dolmen is located an impressively large round barrow at Pant-y-Groes farm. y Gaer is catalogued as an Iron Age hillfort (or Early Medieval - Cambria and RCAHMW No. 304088), the tumulus as a round barrow (RCAHMW No. 304085) of unknown period. Inspection of the relevant section of the 1:25000 OS map shows that these sites are remarkably accurately aligned with Llech y Drybedd, which becomes the third point.

The calculated azimuth from Caer (centre) to Llech y Drybedd is 319° 39'. This was also the major standstill moonset azimuth at this latitude, in 2800 BC. A survey of the three aligned sites was undertaken in 2004.

The perfectly level henge monument known as y Gaer or Caer, as seen from the minor road connecting Felindre Farchog to Moylgrove. From here, the major standstill moonset skimmed the capstone of Llech y Drybedd around 2700 BC

Y Gaer is a raised and fairly level platform which now abuts the minor road that connects Felindre Farchog to Moylgrove. This western edge is covered with a 3m high gorse thicket. The site is some two metres above the present road level, and this drops to half a metre on the eastern curved boundary of the site due to the natural rise of the land. The theodolite survey and subsequent sums showed that y Gaer henge was located precisely such that from the platform, the major standstill moonset in the north would clip the capstone of Llech y Drybedd as it set around 2850 BC.

From Gaer 'B' Azimuth 319°33'

Here are three prehistoric sites in a perfectly linear alignment. That is interesting enough yet has never before been commented on. Apply a little astronomical science and this alignment shows the dolmen and y Gaer to be a lunar observatory from 2800 BC, and this new information helps us to understand with what the people who built these monuments were preoccupied. They were accurately observing the moon and could have predicted eclipses from this site. The provisional survey report is available on www.skyandlandscape.com for those who wish to study or check the full methodology and figures.

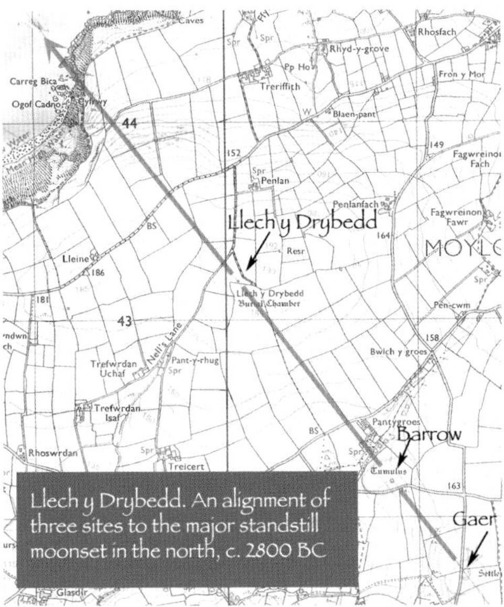

Llech y Drybedd. An alignment of three sites to the major standstill moonset in the north, c. 2800 BC

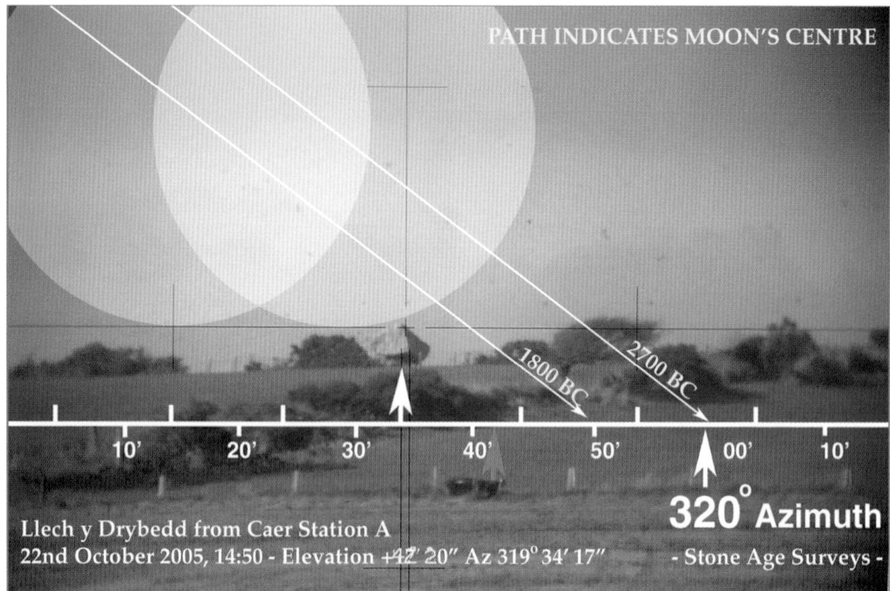

The ultimate test occured in 2006 during the last previous major standstill of the moon. The sums were re-calculated in order to account for the reduction in the angle of the earth's tilt since 2800 BC. This suggested that to see the alignment 'work', as it once clearly did, one would have to walk 86 feet further to the north from y Gaer. So, on the fourth of April 2006, at 2:59 in the morning, I was on the predicted spot armed with a camera and theodolite, and despite 'difficult' weather, I was able to take the photograph shown on the right. I have superimposed Llech's capstone taken from the photo above only to make clear to the reader what is happening, which was a complete test of the validity of this alignment to the extreme moonset in the north.

Llech y Drybedd from Gaer
2:59 am 4/4/2006 (+86 ft)

Carrig Coetan Arthur - Lunar Observatory

Newport's dumpy dolmen offers another glimpse of neolithic ingenuity. The lunar aspects of this site make it very different from Llech y Drybedd, just up the road. Coetan Arthur works by detecting the southern transit of the moon when it is at the major standstill position in the summer. As any outdoor person knows, when the moon is around full in the summer it is always low in the sky, and never more so than when it is at the major standstill period, every 18.6 years. Then, for about a year, it descends to 9 degrees above the horizon when at its monthly minimum declination. This is the lowest that the moon ever crosses the south point.

This is exploited to the full at the dolmen. To the south of Coetan Arthur stands Carningli, its peak leading into the high ground of Carningli Common to the right. The dolmen's location was chosen to match the lunar disc's minimum height to the skyline, when the moon would appear like a glowing silver wheel as it rose up the left-hand edge of Carningli. Then it would disappear into the rocky chaos of the peak (*below, left*), then emerge on the right-hand side and roll along the Common (*below, right*). At any other time in the next 18 years, it would not have performed this trick again.

Major Moon 12/6/2006 2:00 am
from Coetan Arthur

So effective is this design of standstill detector that it is possible to determine when the maximum height of the moon's tiny wobble is occuring, and thereby identify when an eclipse may occur at the next full moon. The total wobble amounts to two-thirds of the diameter of the moon's disc, and detecting when it has reached its maximum is as difficult as recognising when a car wheel is 40 cm off the ground!

To me, what is so good about searching out evidence for prehistoric astronomy is that it has so much to tell us about the thinking abilities of those early astronomers. While archaeologists spend most of their time looking underground for fragments of pottery and the remains of these people, most of what they find amounts to little more than domestic rubbish from whatever period the stratigraphy of the dig corresponds to. This is not to rubbish the work that archaeologists do, which has evidently been vital to date the sites we have considered here. But digging is invasive, often highly destructive and it is very expensive. Looking up into the skies is neither, and has here shed a great deal of light on the intellectual life of the community that once inhabited West Wales.

Maen Corlan Samson Lunar Alignment

The most northerly peak of Carn Meibion Owen (*CMO4 on the photograph on page 88*) acts as a lunar foresight for the minor standstill in the south. The foresight is once again that peculiar 'dodgem car' stone with the headlamps, Maen Corlan Samson. Indeed the holes point to the final outcrop and are visible with the naked eye from there.

I am currently looking at other good solar and lunar sites, but my work is not at a stage where I would want to commit it to paper. However, one of these sites is of relevance here because it blurs the boundaries between an astronomical alignment and a long alignment that runs over miles of territory and where the alignment is not astronomical over most of its length, due to changes in the horizon profile. While from Carn Meibion Owen, we find three sites in alignment - Pentre Ifan, Maen Corlan Samson and Castell Henllys, the midwinter solstice is only accurately valid from the two former sites, because the horizon altitude from Castell Henllys will alter where the sun sets on Carn Meibion Owen. But reverse direction from here and the change in horizon altitude works cleverly such that all the sites *en route* to the horizon, at Cader Idris, indicate the point of the major standstill moonrise in the north. If this could be shown to be intentional, and the evidence here suggests this to be a worthwhile pursuit, then these guys were extremely good at finding just the right locations to enable an alignment to serve two astronomical functions in opposite directions.

Two views from the 'knee' of the northernmost outcrop of Carn Meibion Owen. The left-hand photo shows both Pentre Ifan and Maen Corlan Samson, the right-hand photo was taken through the eyepiece of a theodolite and shows the 'cup-marks'. From this inscribed stone the southern minor standstill moon would set in the 'knee'.

The lunar alignment is observed from Maen Corlan Samson - the solar backsight to Pentre Ifan described on page 88 & 89. Accurate theodolite work revealed that the left-hand 'knee' of this most northerly outcrop on Carn Meibion Owen summit, (whose azimuth measured 229.495 degrees and elevation + 4.588 degrees) was where the minor standstill moonset would have occurred around 3500 BC. The triangular slope of the foresight would enable changes to the moon's wobble to be noticed, again to facilitate the prediction of eclipses. It is nearly rocket science! The fully illustrated survey report is available on the website: www.skyandlandscape.com. Free!

A St Michael Line for Preseli

One alignment that seems to qualify as related to the solar calendar begins at the summit of Foel Eryr and ends on the tip of Strumble Head. It passes through the stones at Trellwyn farm, Parc Y Meirw stone row, the burial chamber on the hill at Penrhiw, above Goodwick, through the church in Llanwnda and on to Strumble Head. Nearby is Carregwastad Point, where over 1,400 French soldiers landed during a pathetically doomed invasion of Britain in 1797. You can find out all about this storm in a teacup in the Royal Oak pub, located in the town square in Fishguard. It's a pantomime story!

The azimuth angle is 117° looking to Foel Eryr from points on the line (*lower right* & *opposite page*). This latter angle corresponds to St Michaels day, May the 8th, which is the start of the third month of Thom's 16 month prehistoric calendar. Our present Mayday or Beltane, on May 1st, is an approximation to the 'cross-quarter' days of the more ancient calendar.

The Parc y Gromlech burial chamber at Penrhiw (*upper right*) has its capstone aligned to the 'St Michael's Day' sunrise from Foel Eryr. The design of this chambered tomb and even the stone from which it is made more resembles the much older dolmens found on the France *causses* than anything found in the Preselis. For a start, it looks inland, to Foel Eryr, clearly visible on the photograph to the right. From the summit and looking the other way, sunset occurs over Strumble Head during Lammas.

The church at Llanwnda has important connections. The famous Welsh chronicler Giraldus Cambrensis was rector here in the 13th Century. It is dedicated to St Gwyndaf, (*gywn* means holy, blessed or white) who was born early in the 6th Century. His father was a refugee from Brittany. Gwyndaf became chaplain of Dyfrig's college in Caerleon about 540 AD and founded Llanwnda church in the mid 6th Century. He was duly ferried across to Bardsey Island to die, in accordance with the custom. The present church, built on the old site and 'restored' in 1881, is of typical Victorian Welsh design, cruciform in shape with a double bellcote. There are six Celtic stone monuments built into the walls and there are four cross-marked stones dating from the 7th to the 9th centuries. One of the window sills has a stone, carved with the image of a cleric holding a staff, once part of a broken stone cross.

Foel Eryr from Strumble Head

The longest line that can be drawn across southern England is that from Land's End to Hopton, near Great Yarmouth in East Anglia. The line incorporates a great many historic, ancient and prehistoric sites along its length. The St Michael line has many tumps, mumps, crags, stone circles (*Avebury*), tors and churches (*Glastonbury*) dedicated to St Michael, the ruler of high places, perched on its high places. Archangel Michael is important in Wales too - Llanfihangel towns and church names are to be found all over this beautiful land.

Strumble Head Lighthouse

Llanwnda Church

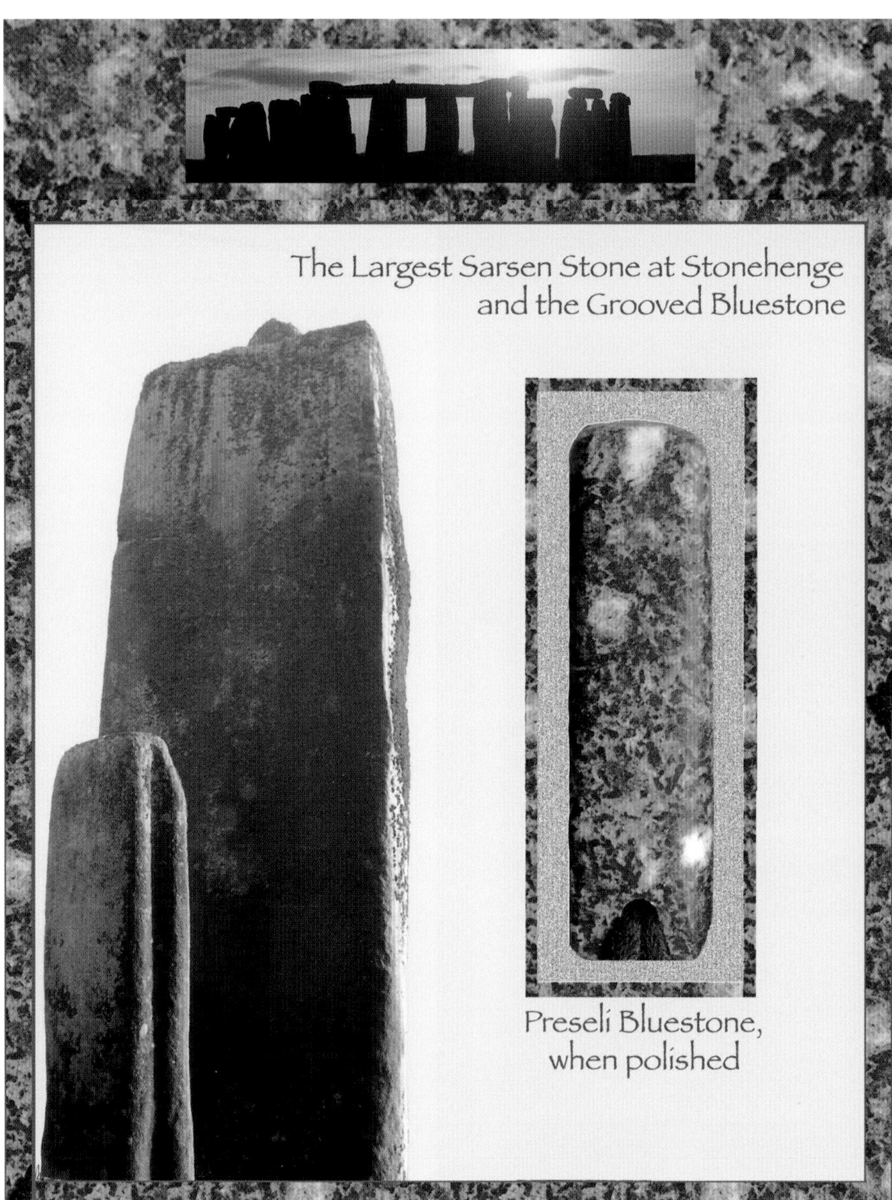

The Largest Sarsen Stone at Stonehenge and the Grooved Bluestone

Preseli Bluestone, when polished

Chapter Five

The Bluestones & Stonehenge
The History of the Mystery

The Preseli region of West Wales is awash with history. From the melting of the last Ice Age to the present day, this beautiful corner of Britain has supported a wide range of different human cultural activities. Much of its history is wrapped in and around these dark and timeless hills like a seemingly impenetrable blanket, its secrets hidden within the many folds of this time-blanket, whose weft is time itself. Central to this is understanding the secret of why the bluestones were so central to Stonehenge, for they were used several times there during a construction that lasted at least 1500 years. *Why*?

It is to the conventional archaeological evidence at Stonehenge that we must now turn in order to establish just what is held there, under the chalk, 'on the premises'. There remains no better book on the archaeology of Stonehenge than Professor Richard Atkinson's classic work *Stonehenge*, first published by Hamish Hamilton in 1956. Written during a year's break in the eight years of excavation, Atkinson in his preface states categorically that the book is designed for the non-specialist reader and is 'not a book for archaeologists, or at least not for those in whose studies Stonehenge must play a significant part.' In this statement, Atkinson was uncharacteristically self-effacing, for the book was and probably still remains amongst the best books on Stonehenge, for professional and non-specialist alike, both in the thoughtfulness and the quality of writing, for anyone who wishes to grasp something of the nature and sequence of the Stonehenge story.

Nor is Atkinson culpable for the chronologial errors which have subsequently been revealed during the fifty years that have elapsed since his book first appeared, just before the science of radiocarbon dating arrived and pushed the chronology further back into the past. The order of construction of the monument nevertheless remains as he proposes and any modern study of prehistory tracks along the same journey through time as Stonehenge itself. Anyone today who attempts to make some sense out of those stones on Salisbury Plain is similarly bound by the limitations of the vision and knowledge of the age in which they find themselves.

Atkinson had a lot to say concerning the bluestones. Primarily he upheld the opinion that they were moved by human action, based on Thomas's work. But he gave much more information about these enigmatic and troublesome stones. His excavations of many of the fifty-six Aubrey holes, provided evidence the 'they were never intended to hold any kind of upright, either the bluestones...or wooden posts', and he gives highly specific and credible evidence for this forthright view. In 1953, the excavations revealed a fragment of freshly fractured bluestone in the deliberate filling around the ditch surrounding the Heel Stone. This 'gives an additional proof of the early presence of the bluestones on the site, for it can be shown that both the Heel Stone and its ditch belong to early phases of the monument'.

Professor Richard Atkinson undertook a systematic excavation and restoration of Stonehenge in the 1950s.

Stone 36 in the Stonehenge classification is a bluestone lintel, and it was excavated, lifted, turned and inspected during the exacavations. It is polished in three dimensions and contains two accurately cut mortice holes and seats for fitting it on top of two uprights in order to provide a bluestone trilithon. In discussing the dressing applied to the bluestones, Atkinson finishes with another remarkable statement, 'In general, the standard of tooling on the dressed bluestones far surpasses even the most careful work on the sarsens; and the finish of certain individual stones, and particularly stone 36 [*see right*], must be accounted among the finest achievements of the mason's craft in prehistoric Europe. It is one of the most curious features of Stonehenge that the art of dressing stones with such skill, and to shapes so aesthetically satisfying, should here have reached so high a pitch, and yet was not imitated, even in the crudest fashion, on any other British monument of later date'.

The bluestone lintel, stone 36. For a few days it rose from the chalk, only to be re-interred.

What is perhaps even more curious is that after this stone was excavated and inspected, it was immediately placed back from whence it had come, so that nobody can have the pleasure of seeing and marvelling at the very best stone on the entire Stonehenge site! Apart from a few black and white photographs (*above*), there is no profile for this stone, and the public remain, like the stone itself, kept in the dark.

Atkinson only found two bluestone lintels on the site, the second one is recumbent but fortunately still visible as part of the north-eastern side of the bluestone circle (stone 152). Several of the larger polished bluestones that now form the pillars of the bluestone horseshoe display the remains of tenons on their tops, two them still possess tenons protuding from their top and these share the same radius as the curved outer surface of the lintel. Of the remainder, Atkinson interestingly writes that, 'In every case where the upper part of a pillar survives intact, its top surface has been dressed flat and level.', implying that the pillar was polished down and modified from an earlier role as a supporting upright for bluestone lintels.

Later in the preface, Atkinson makes the following confession, '..I have not scrupled to indulge in certain speculations, of a kind which my more austere colleagues may well reprehend, upon the possible significance

and interpretation of many aspects of Stonehenge, where the evidence will not bear the full weight of certainty. Silence upon such questions is too frequently justified by an appeal to the strict canons of archaeological evidence, when in fact it merely serves to conceal a lack of imagination.'

Modern chronological and other methods aside, previous models of prehistory, that obeyed the 'strict canons of archaeological evidence' have consistently been shown to be flawed, a truth that led one prehistorian archaeologist, Dr Glyn Daniel (*left*), as the editor of *Antiquity*, to lament that, 'The problem with archaeology is when to stop laughing.' The antiquarian John Michell (*below*) went straight to the point, suggesting that the sum total of archaeologists' attempts to tell us anything much useful concerning why a monument is located where it is and what it may have been used for, has amounted to little more than almost nothing.

Why is this comment so embarrassingly near the truth of the matter? Part of the answer lies in the fact that archaeology, which prides itself on adopting a multi-discipline approach, nevertheless fails in its training of undergraduates to consider the geometry, astronomy and metrology of prehistoric sites. It has held the subject back in a demonstrable way.

By comparison, geological science has, in recent centuries, unlocked many of the secrets held beneath this landscape. The richly varied geology of Pembrokeshire attracts earth scientists from all over the world, each summer bringing large numbers of university groups who discover more or less a total collection of geological ages, minerals and rock formations within a single and rather small county of these islands.

It is in the arena where geology and archaeology meet where the most lively arguments about prehistoric intent are currently raging. It concerns whether the bluestones were moved by human hand to Stonehenge or by the action of glacial flow. The notorious Preseli bluestones were used in the earliest constructions at Stonehenge, around 3000 BC.

This battle of ideas, like this book, has the Preseli region at its very centre. A good overview of this battle may be gleaned from the book *The Bluestone Enigma* by Dr Brian John, a retired lecturer in Geology at Durham University. The modern story of the transportation of the stones from Preseli is less than a century old, before then there was a story told by Merlin of them arriving from Ireland. That glaciation was responsible for the appearance of the stones on Salisbury Plain has never been proven, and perhaps never will be, but neither is there firm evidence that proves human involvement in transporting the stones from Preseli to Salisbury Plain.

To make matters more cloudy, both camps are divided within their own ranks. Many geologists argue that there is no proof of Pleistocene glaciation on Salisbury Plain (from the era of the last Ice Age, which ended around 8000 BCE), and therefore there was no glaciation there at all. However, in 1973, geologist Geoffrey Kellaway suggested the idea that glaciation from the much earlier Pliocene Epoch (5.4 million to 1.6 million years ago) provided a more likely vehicle to have transported the stones to the region. This rekindled the argument and provided further fuel to drive the bluestone debate into present times.

Merlin's Story - Geoffrey of Monmouth's Tale

The idea that the stones at Stonehenge were transported over a large distance began in the twelfth century. The first reference to this subject comes from Geoffrey of Monmouth, who in an epic story informed his readers concerning the building of Stonehenge. He wrote that when Merlin suggested to King Aurelius that he should send an expedition to Ireland to collect the stones from Mount Killaraus, the King burst out with laughter, asking, "how can such large stones be moved from so far distant a country?" Not an unreasonable response today, one might think.

Merlin was irritated by the King's response. He rebukes the King for his 'foolish laughter', and goes on to say that "what I say has nothing ludicrous about it. These stones are connected with certain secret religious rites and they have various properties which are medicinally important. Many years ago the Giants transported them from the remotest confines of Africa and set them up in Ireland at a time when they inhabited that country."

Geoffrey is not remembered as the most accurate chronicler of his time. However, this story contains a kernel of truth in that, during the fifth century, there was indeed an emperor or war-lord whose name was Aurelianus. Ambrosius Aurelianus took on the mantle of a Romano-British 'king' and fought against the Saxon advances, culminating in the battle of Badon Hill, a battle which, according to Gildas, gave forty years of peace in the midst of perhaps the most turbulent period in Britain's entire history. Although never mentioned by Gildas, Arthur became identified as the legendary victor at Badon Hill.

Geoffrey's story is contemporary with his lifetime and yet he relates it from a fifth century perspective. The King in Geoffrey's story is clearly possessed of a Dark Age mind-set. By the twelfth century no medieval King would have laughed at the idea of importing large stones from overseas when such had already become standard practice for large building works. Many of Britain's finest cathedrals and monasteries were built or were being built using stone imported by boat from all over Britain and Europe, particularly from France. Is Geoffrey's story then a recounting of an otherwise lost legend about the source of the Stonehenge stones, set in an earlier period of British history when Aurelius's response would have been entirely appropriate?

Merlin's insistence that the stones were taken from Ireland also benefits from being looked at from a fifth century viewpoint. In southwest Wales, Merlin's birthplace was allegedly Carmarthen (Caer Myrddin) in Dyfed, the same area where Herbert Thomas demonstrated that the Stonehenge bluestones had originated. The western parts of the region had been colonised in the fifth century by an Irish tribe, the Deisi. From the perspective of the fifth century, Ireland was not totally confined to that large island across the Irish sea that we identify with the country today. The Deisi established a dynasty of Irish Kings in West Wales, whose rule was to endure in the region until at least the tenth century, after which the Vikings increasingly broke their grip on the region. In consequence the local spoken language for five centuries was Irish and several town names offer confirmation of this. For example, the Welsh name of Moylgrove, near Cardigan, is Trewyddel, which means 'Irish town'. And on the bank of the Nhyfer river north of Pentre Ifan lies Wern Gwyddel, 'Irish Croft'.

Further evidence that this region was indeed 'Irish' may be found from the wealth of surviving standing stones in the region that are inscribed with Ogham script, a 'language' which originated from Ireland. The practice of inscribing local gravestones with the word 'maqi', meaning 'son of', rather than the Welsh 'mab' or 'ap' further supports a linguistic demonstration of the Irish historical presence in the region. Both these practices can still be be 'read' from stones all held within the curtilage of Nevern Church, near Newport, and its churchyard, whose entrance is lined with ancient Irish yews. The practice of planting yews in English churchyards only originated with Edward I at the beginning of the fourteenth century. [for more on Ogham stones in Wales, see John Sharkey's book, *Ogham Monuments in Wales*]

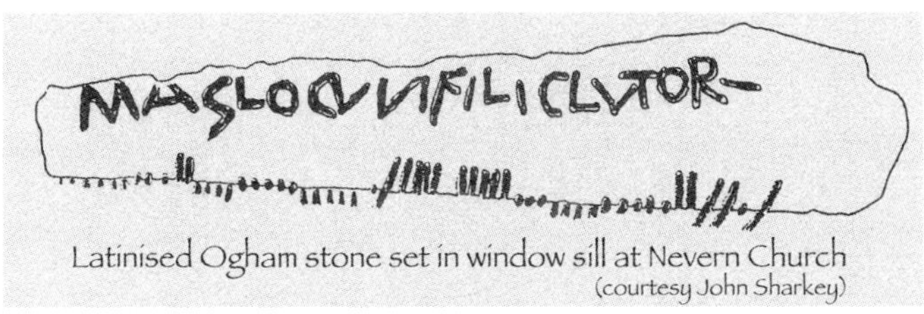

Latinised Ogham stone set in window sill at Nevern Church
(courtesy John Sharkey)

The Nevern site is therefore the quintessential example of Irish influence in Wales during the period from the fifth to the tenth century. Nevern is two miles from Pentre Ifan and six miles from the source of the bluestones. Also of interest is that the Romans never took control of West Wales. According to Ptolemy, a much more reliable chronicler than Geoffrey of Monmouth ever was, it remained the territory of the Demetae, a local tribe. It was presumably held by them until the Irish arrived in the fifth century.

So Merlin's story can be understood in the light of important but limited historical facts to explain his 'Irish' source for the stones taken to build Stonehenge. The obvious flaw in this argument is seldom if ever given the importance it deserves. The stones being referred to in Merlin's story are, of course, the huge sarsens that make up the much, much larger Sarsen circle and the five trilithons erected within it around the centre of Stonehenge. These stones were, since about 2700 BC, the visual essence of the monument, and remain so to this day. They are its logo. They are the stones depicted in the crude medieval woodcut showing Merlin's giants at work erecting a square Stonehenge!

The sarsens came from much more local source, under 20 miles away from Fyfield down, near Avebury on the Marlborough downs. Some weigh in at over 50 tons and one is 22 feet tall, and they inevitably steal the show, distracting attention away from the much smaller bluestones, which, in comparison weigh in at no more than four tons and are at best seven feet tall. These diminutive stones remain of little concern to a casual visitor at Stonehenge today, as one may safely assume that they would have done to a fifth century war-lord in Merlin's time.

The bluestones were however the first dressed stones to be employed in the construction that became Stonehenge, long before the sarsens were placed in their circle and the five trilithons were placed around the central area. Is it credible that Merlin was recounting an epic stone moving episode from around 3000 BC, some four thousand years later? In *The White Goddess*, Robert Graves suggests that an original stone circle was taken to Stonehenge during later prehistoric times, but there is no evidence to fall back on and we reach a historical dead end. No one has ever found evidence for this circle. We must ask if it is realistic that Merlin or anyone else in the fifth century would know of such a prehistoric transfer of stones from Wales ('Ireland') to Wessex? It stretches druidic oral tradition beyond its limit when the time difference may be 3500 years, or 300 generations. Support for such a cultural continuation has to be understood as a last ditch attempt to shore up a weak argument, and more evidence is required if Geoffrey's story is ever to be regarded as other than a fanciful early medieval yarn.

However, another slant can be taken on the argument. What Merlin does in Geoffrey's story is inform the listener concerning a remote source of stones being employed at Stonehenge. Dr Herbert Thomas subsequently identified one location from where a remote source of stone was indeed employed at Stonehenge, making this aspect of Merlin's story impressively correct. Since 1923, we have known that a distant source of stones was employed. We also know that Merlin was brought up in the same region of Wales from where these stones originated. If Merlin indeed knew of a tradition concerning the source of stones from the Preselis to Stonehenge, we may never be able to find any other evidence for it, but we do now know that these stones ended up at Stonehenge.

We now face another possibility. If the actual location of the bluestone site held an inherent significance to Stonehenge's meaning, and this meaning had remained known about and culturally important long after the bluestones had been taken to Stonehenge, glacially or otherwise, then Geoffrey via Merlin could have been aware of a fifth century legend drawing attention to this in his story to King Aurelius. And even if we dismiss the whole Geoffrey of Monmouth episode as irrelevant, there is nothing to stop anyone investigating whether the location of the bluestone site is related in some other way with Stonehenge, a task that has been my preoccupation for some years.

The Merlin in Geoffrey's story spoke Welsh, the language spoken throughout most of Britain until the Anglo-Saxon makeover, and Merlin was also contemporary with the Irish occupation of south-west Wales. To him, as for later Saxon and Viking occupants of these lands, the Preseli mountains would have been understood as being part of Ireland. As for the location of Mount Killaraus, as no one is certain where this is, and as we now know that the stones did not come from Ireland proper, future speculation as to origins in Ireland would appear futile. But not if they originated from Wales.

Put the two Welsh words Cil and arlais together and one gets 'corner temple', Cil and arhosol yields 'abiding retreat'. Etymological fun, but no help in identifying the location of Mount Killaraus either! However, if Merlin also spoke Irish and was the clever man we are led to believe he was, then Cill or Kill is the Irish for church or temple, while arlais is Welsh for temple, making Mount Killaraus 'Mount church temple' or, put more simply, 'Sacred Mountain'. Richard Atkinson wrote that he thought the Preselis were seen by the late Neolithic beaker folk to be a 'sacred mountain', a place from which they could survey the major trading routes by both land and sea. To do this they would have needed excellent eyesight.

In 1655, a book was published posthumously which made direct comment on the Merlin story. The King's architect Inigo Jones (1573-1652) had written about Stonehenge, 'The same kind of Stone whereof this Antiquity consists, may be found, especially about Aibury (*Avebury*) in North-Wiltshire, not many miles distant from it, where are not only quarries of the like stone, but also stones of far greater dimensions then any at Stonehenge, may be had.'

Jones is here referring to the giant sarsen stones, which came from Fyfield Down, just two miles east of Avebury, and he then mocks the Merlin story, 'For, as for that ridiculous Fable, of Merlin's transporting the stones out of Ireland by Magick, it is an idle conceit'.

George Owen's Tale

Curiously, it was a native of Pembrokeshire who became the acknowledged father figure of the emerging science of Geology. George Owen was a product of the very beginning of the Age of Enlightenment, being born at Henllys, near Nevern, in1552. Later he was to become a progressive farmer, and began the practice of introducing natural mineral fertilisers to the soil. Later in his life he became the first person to understand the geology of Pembrokeshire and to demonstrate that the same types of rock were normally to be found in the same sequence or strata wherever they were found. As a consequence of this endeavour he produced the first decent map of the county, so good that it was chosen for *Britannia*, the classic work by William Camden, an essential book within the library of all well to do folk from the eighteenth century onwards.

The *Edinburgh Review* referred to Owen as the 'Patriarch of English Geologists', this showing that the Scots were just as culpable of lumping Wales with England four centuries ago as many English people annoyingly persist in doing today. However, it is also true that Owen was determined to be seen as belonging to the Normans, having married well to Elizabeth Philips, daughter of William and Janet Philips of Picton Castle, and he held a number of offices of high bearing within the county, being at one time or another, a Justice of the Peace, Deputy Lieutenant, Sheriff and Deputy Vice-Admiral for both Cardigan and Pembrokeshire.

George Owen became an influential figure within the rising Elizabethan interest in antiquities, and widely supported and contributed to scholarship and learning in this field. In 1603 he wrote his master work on his findings, as *Description of Pembrokeshire*, first published in popular format only in 1892. As we shall later discover, George Owen made some very astute observations concerning the prehistoric monuments contained within the Preseli region.

There is a brass plaque dedicated to George Owen and sited directly behind the pulpit in Nevern Church. Well worn through centuries of polishing, it reads:

TO THE GLORY and famous memory of GEORGE OWEN of Henllys in this parish, Lord of Kemes (Cemaes), who died on the 26th of August 1612 (recte 1613) aged 61 years. He was a Justice of the peace, a Deputy Lieutenant and deputy Vice Admiral of this county and twice served the office of High Sheriff. He was zealous in the performance of all his public duties and in the promotion of the various interest of his native county. He has been styled Patriarch of English Geologists; by his Description of Pembrokshire, and his other works on the history and antiquities of this county and of the Principality of Wales, he has raised an imperishable monument of his singular learning and industry to his own high renown and to the honour of his beloved county of Pembroke.

George Owen occupied himself making the first study of the geology of Pembrokeshire; a modern geological map makes it apparent there was much to keep him occupied! The Preseli Hills divides itself into two main geological regions. That region south of a line from the Nevern River Estuary to Carn Wen is predominantly made up of igneous dolerite rocks that form a coastal band down to St Davids, while north of this line one finds the evidence for more recent, in a geological sense, disturbed volcanic activity.

Owen's interest in the prehistoric monuments of the county placed him uniquely as the first to connect archaeology with geology, and this adds to one of the most enduring mysteries connecting this region with Britain's most famous prehistoric monument, our National Temple, Stonehenge.

In the important matter of the bluestone's relationship with Stonehenge, there is useful evidence from the sixteenth century. A remarkable comment was made by George Owen, over four centuries ago, referring to Pentre Ifan. He wrote,

> '*The stone called Maen y Gromlech upon Pentre Ifan land,.. (is).. a huge and massive stone mounted on high and set on the tops of three other high stones pitched standing upright in the ground. It far surpasses for bigness and height... any other that I ever saw, saving some at Stonehenge..*'

In other words, as far back as 1603, Owen made the first tenous link between Preseli bluestone and Stonehenge, perhaps without realising the significance of his comments. We may speculate that, as a geologist also interested in the ancient monuments of Pembrokeshire, he would surely have carried his geological hammer with him on his travels and have chipped small pieces off both monuments in order to identify the stones and make the comparison. And surely he must have recognised the similarity between the bluestones at Stonehenge and those of his native county, particularly as the stones from which Pentre Ifan is constructed are the same dolerite as the larger Stonehenge bluestones, albeit less ophitic (spotted) with quartz. It is even possible to speculate that Owen was, like Merlin, drawing veiled attention to arcane knowledge concerning a great secret connecting the bluestone site with Stonehenge, a secret to which we will return later.

The Geologist's Tale - Herbert Thomas

In the early 1920s, another distinguished Welsh geologist and petrologist, Dr Herbert Thomas, presented to the Society of Antiquaries a report that the eponymous bluestones had originated from a 2Km square area centred on Carn Menyn. Today, these same stones may be seen at Stonehenge as a 75 foot diameter stone circle once comprising perhaps 60 bluestones, together with a 38 foot diameter 'horseshoe' or ellipse of nineteen elegant and finely polished bluestone pillars. Using petrological analysis, Thomas's published paper in 1923 appeared to finally identify unequivocally from where these stones had come, although not how they had arrived at Stonehenge. Thomas, unaware of the extent of glaciation in previous epochs, naturally placed his bet, perhaps rather too firmly, on the side of human transportation being the reason for the bluestone's presence at Stonehenge.

Thomas concluded that it was from a remarkably localised region of the Preseli mountains that many of the bluestones found at Stonehenge originated. These were utilised in various aspects of the monument's design, from the very earliest constructions, and they finally ended up being reused during the very final stages of the monument's evolution being placed inside and alongside the more massive (and much more local) sarsen circle.

Since Thomas's work, spirited and sometimes fierce and occasionally acrimonious debate periodically erupts within academic circles in an attempt to answer this key question: Did the bluestones arrive on Salisbury Plain through the actions of glacial flow during the last Ice Age, or were they delivered at huge expense of human effort over land and water? Both options spawn further questions. If glacial flow delivered the bluestones, then why did only about eighty of them arrive on Salisbury Plain, with apparently almost no other glacial debris? And as most of the bluestones are of about the same size, there has been a tendency to assume that these were somehow 'chosen', hand-picked stones, rather than mere litter from glacial melting. If, however, they were man-handled to Stonehenge, these eighty-odd stones, some as big as four tons, had to have been hauled over a distance of hundreds of miles. The direct distance from the bluestone outcrop at Carn Menyn to Stonehenge is 135 miles (220 km) as the raven flies. And the biggest question of all is why they should even have undertaken such a Herculean task when perfectly good sarsen stone was available, and indeed was utilised, from a source very much nearer to the monument they were constructing?

Some dismiss Thomas's work as less than rigorous, and often have an agenda to support the glacial theory or to reduce the possibilities that Stonehenge is more than a roughly built pile of stones. One thing is however true. Each side of the argument, whether sourced from academic or popular writings, has produced its own mythology on the subject. The glaciation group produce an argument that is largely comprised of showing that the human movement of stones would be unlikely if not impossible, while those that favour human transportation have failed to furnish evidence of how the task was achieved. The 'moved by man' supporters have failed to answer another vital question - *why it was necessary to move bluestones from Preseli to Stonehenge in the first place*? The glacial theory folk have not answered why the builders of Stonehenge spent dozens of man-years dressing super-hard bluestones when they had a ready source of a much more malleable rock just north of Stonehenge. These are the vitally important questions and they have not been satisfactorily answered.

Amongst modern archaeologists, Geoffrey Wainwright and Timothy Darvill have resuscitated the old medieval chestnut of an earlier Geoffrey and suggested that the (alleged) healing properties of the bluestones provided the impetus to make transporting over eighty of them to Stonehenge sufficiently important to warrant all the sweat and toil that task would entail. One feels it would have been easier and healthier for the tribes on Salisbury Plain just simply to move to Preseli instead! At least this new theory attempts to answer why the bluestones were transported, with little supporting evidence. Meanwhile, another archaeologist, Aubrey Burl, our most senior archaeology expert on stone rings, writes eloquently on the 'persistent myth' of the human transportation hypothesis. And so it goes on. And on!

The geologists are equally divided. In 1903, twenty years before Thomas identified the source of the bluestones, Professor William Judd was the first to suggest a glacial transport mechanism for the bluestones, not through direct evidence but by suggesting some anomalies in the counter argument that human intent moved the stones,

> *'The old tradition concerning Stonehenge, that it consisted of a circle of 'bluestones' which had acquired a certain sanctity in a distant locality, and had been transported from the original home of the tribe. If so, the stones, brought from so far away, would have been reduced to something like half their bulk … Is it conceivable that these skilful builders would have transported such blocks of stone in their rough state over mountains, hills and rivers (and possibly over seas) in order to shape them at the point of erection?'*

Since Judd's time, various excavations at Stonehenge have found what has become known as the 'Stonehenge floor' or 'Bluestone layer', a stratified collection of tens of thousands of chippings of bluestones below the chalk which confirm that these fine hard stones were dressed and in some cases polished on site at Stonehenge. The stones were dressed at their final destination. A fact! Brian John even suggests that the reason for this was that the locally strewn bluestones, having been gifted to the region by the earlier action of glacial activity, made the place a natural centre for the production of bluestone stone axes. Logic would dictate that the Preseli region would clearly have taken that role, playing Tesco to a corner shop. Transporting small pieces of bluestone to dress them into axes at Stonehenge isn't a sensible option either, although it would have been a lot easier.

The man who started the whole thing, Herbert Thomas, a member of the Geological Survey team, wrote in 1923 that,

> *'..a hypothetical ice sheet, in order to account for the foreign stones of Stonehenge would have to gather from Pembrokeshire blocks all of about the same size and mainly of two rock types. It would have to carry them all that distance without dropping any by the way. Further, it would have to pass over all kinds of rocky obstacles without gathering to itself any of the various materials over which it was forced to ride. Such in itself, without the additional positive evidence that is forthcoming as to the extent of the glaciation of Pembrokeshire and adjoining counties, permanently disposes of the idea of glacial transport for the foreign stones at Stonehenge.'*

Through this statement, Thomas inadvertently threw a huge weight on the scales that have subsequently tipped to uphold the modern myth that human transportation of the bluestones must have taken place. In 2008, Dr John, a geologist himself, describes Thomas's paper as,

> *'remarkably vague and unsatisfactory in many respects; we have no idea, to this day, how many samples he looked at and whether he reported ALL of his analyses. He was driven by the belief that all of the stones must have come from one small source area, as suggested initially by Sir Jethro Teall. So, although some of his rock identifications were anomalous, he seemed unprepared to consider the possibility that they had come from other far distant sources.'*

'In the grand tradition of Stonehenge studies, confidence and bluster were sufficient to overcome any shortcomings on the data front. The five pairs of thin sections which illustrated his article were obviously selected to give the best 'matches' possible [between Stonehenge bluestones and those from Preseli - author's addition]; but that is fair enough, since he, as an author, was seeking to make a case. And let's not be too critical here. Thomas was writing in 1923 when the science of geology was anything but mature, and there is no doubt that his work was of great importance.'

Long before these recent comments, from a committed glaciologist, the cracks in Thomas's argument had already begun. In 1971, Geoffrey Kellaway, a later officer of the Geological Survey, placed new evidence on the table to suggest that an ice sheet had indeed moved up the Bristol Channel and deposited stoney debris into parts of Somerset. In response to this report, W A Cummins, a high profile geologist at St Andrews, previously a senior lecturer in Geology at the University of Nottingham writes,

' There is, however, no evidence of any glacial deposits on Salisbury Plain and the deposits in Somerset are thin and carry no large boulders... In short, the glacial deposits of Somerset gave little reason for revising the conclusions of Thomas regarding the glacial origin of the Stonehenge bluestones.'

Cummings further weakens the glacial argument in his book *King Arthur's Place in Prehistory* (Sutton Publishing, 1992). He asks why an ice sheet should only have deposited eighty or so stones of roughly of the same size onto Salisbury Plain. He pours scorn on Kellaway's implication that there 'may be up to 5000 tons of medium to large erratics hidden away in unexcavated long barrows on Salisbury Plain', reckoning this to 'be clutching at archaeological straws'. He points out that any ice sheet crossing Pembrokeshire would pass over many outcrops of potential bluestones, but that the vast majority of these would not be the spotted variety found at Stonehenge. In a rare and informed grasp of the questions that need to be asked concerning this subject, Cummins wrote,

'It is necessary to consider three questions which concerned Kelloway and others who have favoured the glacial transport hypothesis:

1. Why did the builders of Stonehenge go all the way to Mynydd Preselau for the bluestones, when there were perfectly satisfactory stones to be had much nearer to home?

2. Why, if the main source of bluestone was Mynydd Preselau, did they also bring a single huge block of micaceous sandstone (the greenstone or altar stone at Stonehenge), which certainly did not come from that area?

3. Why, when they were up on Mynydd Preselau, did they sometimes collect such inferior rocks as the altered volcanic ash which has decayed so badly at Stonehenge, when they could just as easily have brought spotted dolerite every time?

Question one suggests that the transporters thought the stones from Preseli were special in some way. Question two makes us consider that the unique Altar stone at Stonehenge, which is thought by many to have originated from near Milford Haven, came from a location (almost at sea level) that was most likely never covered in glacial ice during the last glacial maximum. Question three makes us recognise a crucial aspect of this whole debate that has yet to command the attention it warrants - *it may have been the location itself and not specifically the type of stone from that location that needed to be identified with Stonehenge*, for whatever reasons.

Archaeologist Aubrey Burl has lent support for the glaciation argument, providing much needed archaeological evidence to refute those who have previously suggested that after 3000 BC, gold and copper prospectors returning from a mission in the Wicklow Hills in Ireland became enchanted with locally held ideas that the bluestones were possessed of healing qualities and,

'felt compelled to plunder them one by one for an intended megalithic sanctuary on Salisbury Plain. The romance has been repeated so many times in so many books that it has almost become fact.'

Except that it isn't a fact. Burl then goes on to point out a chronological fault-line held within this modern myth,

'But there is no substance to the story. The early third millennium BCE, when the great monument of Stonehenge was begun, was a pre-metal age which had little contact between Wales and Ireland. That came only with the discovery of Irish copper ores around 2500 BCE. Even then, there is no evidence for prospectors from mainland Britain visiting Ireland. What Irish gold or copper did reach Bronze-Age Wessex probably arrived in the form of ready-made axes and lunulae manufactured in Ireland and carried overseas by Irish traders.'

Professor Judd noted that the people that moved these larger sarsen sandstones 'would appear to have left only the final dressing to be done after their transport', despite moving them only one seventh of the distance of the smaller bluestones. But this is not the case, considerable dressing of the sarsens must have taken place at Stonehenge because over a thousand sarsen mauls used to dress these large stones were used as packing to steady them after they were raised up in their socket holes. Although some of the sarsens weigh in at over 50 tons, making their transport far more problematical, their final dressing, as for the bluestones, took place at the monument - they too were transported roughly dressed.

What are we left with following this look at the various aspects of each side of this debate? In fact, quite a useful amount of information. All the participants in the bluestone debate, from Geoffrey of Monmouth to Geoffrey Wainwright, via George Owen and Herbert Thomas, have produced one common outcome - they have repeatedly drawn our attention to a legend concerning the source of the stones at Stonehenge. Before we dismiss the legend, the recurrence of the theme of this legend is remarkably persistent. No less an author than Alan Garner reminds us, concerning legend, that,

> '*We are dealing with legend, and legend is belief of truth. It is not fiction. It is not imagination. It is reportage.*'

Whether moved by human hand or by glacial action we now know that the majority of large bluestones at Stonhenge - twenty-seven stones - are ophitic (spotted) dolerite and that these originated from north-west of Salisbury Plain, i.e. Wales or Ireland. History informs us that in Merlin's time the Preseli Region *was* Irish and may easily have been thought of as Ireland by someone living in southern England. Both lie across the water to the north west, one across the Bristol Channel, the other across the Irish sea.

Dr Thomas suggested that the bulk of the bluestones came from within 2Km of Carn Meini. He added his own 'reportage' and is therefore as much a part of the legend as was Geoffrey of Monmouth, or Geoffrey of Bournemouth. While other specialist geologists have greatly widened this focus and made all researchers on Stonehenge aware that a large number of other types of rock are also to be found within the collection of structures that are collectively referred to as Stonehenge, the legend today remains firmly focussed on Preseli as the source.

The whole bluestone debate makes us acutely aware that we actually know remarkably little about Stonehenge's purpose. Beneath the apparently calm and ultra conservative archaeology profession foams a frothing morass of contradictory evidence, polemic and intellectual confusion. Stonehenge 'sells' and has become sexy. Fuelled by the popularity of many television documentaries about the monument, most of which reveal nothing new, this profession presently holds a monopoly on the subject. Evidence arriving from other sources is too frequently dismissed as irrelevant, largely because it is threatening to current archaeological beliefs. The popular tag, 'loony fringe' is too often applied to those who propose an alternative viewpoint.

Most of the popularisation of Stonehenge study by the media is both extremely unhealthy and profoundly discouraging for any type of debate or for prospects of obtaining a better understanding of the megalithic builders and their cultural goals. It offers no hope whatever for those who think that the present model of prehistoric life currently presented by archaeology is both inaccurate and incomplete, and is a total insult to our ancestors.

It is an ideal time for some new evidence, drawn from a totally different source. Richard Atkinson discovered that the earliest stone construction at Stonehenge was of bluestones, and this impelled me to look for a connection between Stonehenge and the Preseli bluestone region, independent of the geology and archaeology. My question became:

What if the two locations rather than the stones from those locations were telling us something about why Stonehenge is located where it is?

An article about more recent aspects of the bluestone debate can be found and a PDF file on the website,

www.skyandlandscape.com.

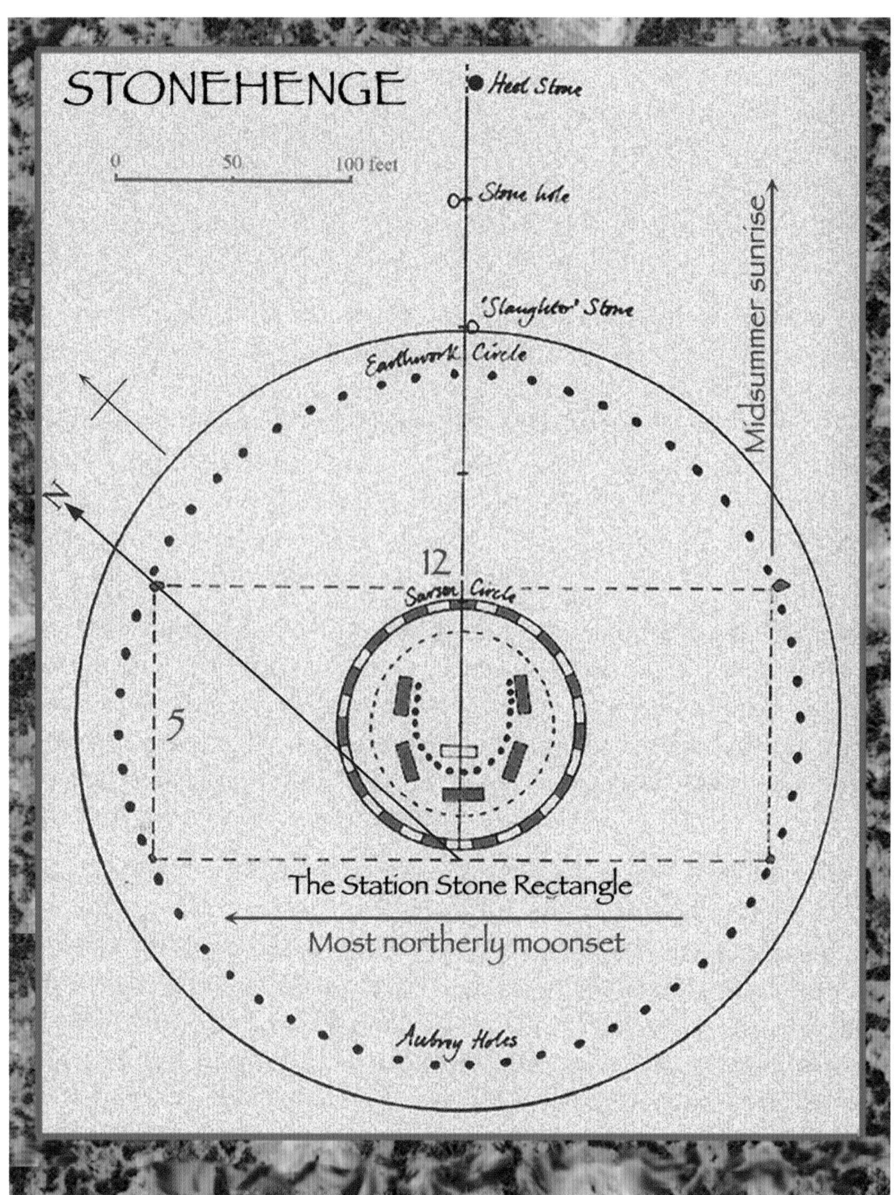
STONEHENGE
0 50 100 feet
Heel Stone
Stone hole
'Slaughter' Stone
Earthwork Circle
Midsummer sunrise
N
12
Sarsen Circle
5
The Station Stone Rectangle
Most northerly moonset
Aubrey Holes

Chapter Six

Bluestone Magic
How Preseli talks to Stonehenge

Stonehenge is physically comprised of circles and horseshoe shaped arcs of circles. The only straight lines are the two banks of the Avenue, aligned to the midsummer sunrise around 3000 BC and the four stones around the perimeter of the Aubrey circle that define an accurate rectangle. The former feature is astronomical, the second is primarily geometrical, although by virtue of its placement within the axis of Stonehenge, the shorter sides of this rectangle also point to the midsummer sunrise while the longer sides point to the major standstill moon rise in the north. These facts were discovered first by Peter Newham and then Professor Thom in the early 60s and then included in the best selling *Stonehenge Decoded* book, written by astronomer Professor Gerald Hawkins and predictably slammed by the archaeologists.

That a right angle defines the two positions of the most northerly sunrise and moonrise at this unique latitude is of much interest here. The theoretical latitude where this is true lies about 30 miles south of Stonehenge, in the Solent, but the horizon elevations at Stonehenge also make it true here. So inside the bank and ditch we have a structure that is both geometrical and astronomically active (*schematic plan opposite*).

The rectangle has sides in the ratio of 5:12, making the diagonals 13 of the same unit, which turn out to be eight of Thom's Megalithic yards. His published figures for the diameter of the Aubrey circle, based on a closed traverse survey, are 283.6 feet, division of this figure by Thom's value for the Megalithic yard (2.72 feet) gives the answer 104.26, which, divided by 8, is 13.03. This makes the '12' side 12.03, and the '5' side 5.01 in units of 8 MY.

After five millenia, this result remains within one part in 1200 of being an perfect rectangular structure - a 99% accurate geometry.

The rectangle implied by the station stones can be thought of as two 5:12:13 right angled triangles. This is the second of the pythagorean triangles, the first being the 3:4:5. What is so special about pythagorean triangles? For a start they are right angled triangles where *all three sides are made up of whole numbers*. Secondly, they can be laid out on the ground using a rope marked into equal divisions. If the middle side ('12') is pegged down, then bringing the ends of the rope together automatically makes the right angle (*see right*), making these triangles very popular with builders throughout history wishing to make an accurate corner in a house, temple or swimming pool.

To find such a triangle framing the middle of Stonehenge says two things, that Pythagoras was a latecomer to this technique, born two thousand years after that rectangle was placed at Stonehenge, and that its builders were familiar with its application, for the corners of the rectangle are squarer than an average modern building. Keeping it simple, the information emerging from this construction is that the builders *were* using the Megalithic yard, as multiples, and that the 5:12:13 structure was important, for around the Aubrey circle they could have placed any other proportion of rectangle, even a square.

I decided to experiment with a rope and pegs and attempt to build a full size replica of the shape in a field adjacent to where I lived. I marked thirty equal divisions of eight Megalithic yards onto a rope, and created a 5:12:13 triangle, marking its corners with bright orange dayglo pegs. I constructed a second identically sized triangle sharing the '13' side of the first one, to form the rectangle. Using surveyor's tapes I then found out that my first attempt had achieved an accuracy of better than part in 1200, and the worst departure from a square corner was 89.7 degrees.

This first version was very large, and the ropes weighed so heavy that it needed two people to carry them. My next move was to reduce the scale to one eighth, and make the 5:12:13 in units of a single Megalithic yard. It was using this version on a local beach when an interesting discovery was made.

The station stone rectangle relates to the local astronomy of the sun and moon at Stonehenge. I began to make an attempt to understand the link between the astronomy and this geometry, as clearly someone had once done at Stonehenge. What followed changed my prespective on the past.

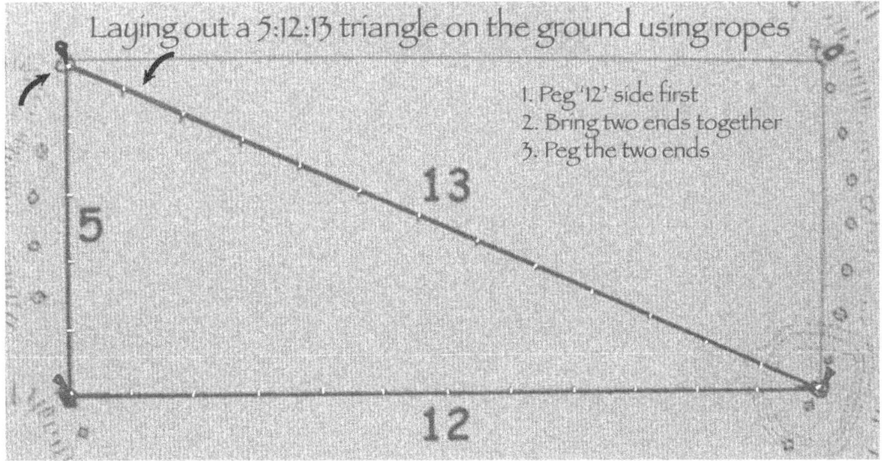
Laying out a 5:12:13 triangle on the ground using ropes
1. Peg '12' side first
2. Bring two ends together
3. Peg the two ends
13
5
12

The Sacred Marriage of the Sun & Moon

In an earlier chapter I showed how prehistoric people could have known the length of the year to the nearest day in a single year, and to within a fraction of an hour in four years, using natural and humanly built devices found in the Preseli hills. The lunar month, the cycle of the phases and also of the tides, is a visual feast that enables an observer to quite accurately define the moment of new moon, when the first thin sliver of the crescent moon appears in the dusk sky shortly after sunset. In one year I was able to define the lunation period as being 29.5 days in length, just noting whenever possible that first sliver in the sky. Some of these I missed, because clouds obscured the moon, but the resulting gap was obvious, and could readily be accounted for. This gave me an accuracy of almost 99.9%.

I began to experience the lunation rather than read off its precise period from an astronomy book. I saw that there were more than 12 lunations in a (solar) year and less than 13 of them. Somewhere between twelve and thirteen moons lay the precise fractional number of lunations in one year. I used simple maths to calculate what 365 (days) divided by 29.5 (days) would be and 12.37 was the answer. Then I took a geometrical short cut. I marked the 12.37 lunation length - which represented the solar year length - onto the '13' side of my triangle and then pivoted it down onto the shortest '5' side from the sharp end of the triangle to find our where it touched. The answer was unexpected - it touched precisely at the '3'-point marker.

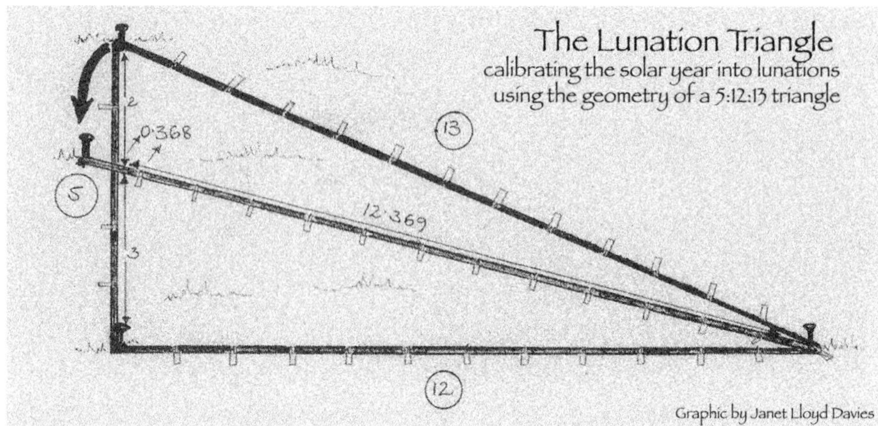

I then went through a very strange few days. This triangle was clearly marrying the two seemingly unrelated cycles of the sun and moon using simple geometry and whole numbers. The geometry married the 365.242 days of the solar year to the 29.53 days of the lunar month. The cosmos was ordered! Whether or not megalithic astronomers had discovered this device, it solved the problem of building a soli-lunar calendar! What I had actually recognised was that I had found an unbelievably simple, accurate and portable tool for doing the job. The new long side or hypotenuse is ready calibrated to the solar year in lunations (lunar months), and this had been achieved using just a long rope marked out with thirty equal divisions (that made up the required 5 + 12 + 13 lengths).

From then on, placing me anywhere on the planet with a rope or rods, within a couple of hours I could produce a working calendar with all the full, new and even quarter moons arranged on the correct day of the coming year, even two or three years, and these would be to the day. The device used to perform this calendrical feat I named the Lunation Triangle.

Secrets of the Lunation Triangle

Because the original idea had come from the station rectangle at Stonehenge, I had marked up prototype ropes using the Megalithic yard as the distance between each marker. This length represented one lunar month of 29.53 days. I discovered that when one does this, the extra 11 days between the end of 12 lunar months and the end of a solar year was another familar measure - unbelievably so it seemed at the time, it was one English foot in length. And that wasn't all, because the construction leaves another well known ancient measure outside of the triangle - the Royal cubit. A foot ruler can be seen on the photograph to the right. The Megalithic yard is seen to equal the foot plus the Royal cubit.

Three of the most ancient units of length known to us today are seen to be proportionally related to the way the sun and the moon move in the sky. The rectangle at Stonehenge was laid out using the Megalithic yard, suggesting that its builders may have known all about this device, while our present culture apparently no longer knows or cares much concerning these kinds of enquiry. The moon has become a lifeless satellite, it's motion seen as annoyingly capricious and misaligned to solar realities. The lunation triangle shows how to re-integrate the moon's cycles within the solar year.

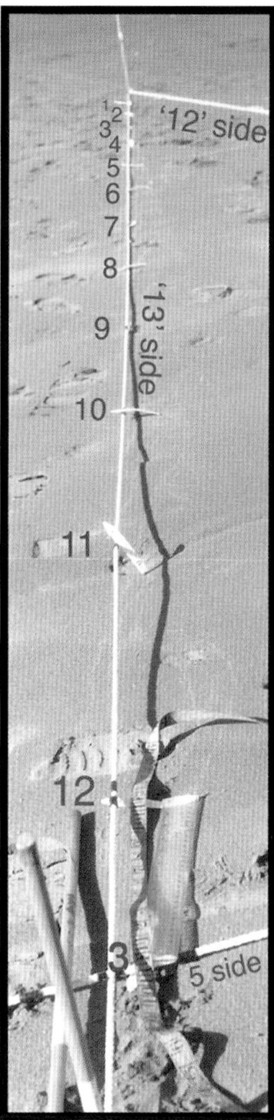

The 3:2 point on a lunation triangle constructed on a beach. 12.368 lunar months - the solar year - is calibrated in months of 29.53 days to high accuracy.

A Beautiful Geometry

New ideas take time to be assimulated. I had entered the mind of a neolithic astronomer and this brought with it some readjustments to the way I saw our modern culture, which now appeared more and more to be over complicated, and out of touch with the rhythms of the sky. We no longer dance to the music of the spheres and therefore our culture is no longer aligned to the cosmos.

How is it possible for knowledge of this technique to have become forgotten? I trawled libraries of ancient books to try to find a reference to it *anywhere*. The best I came up with is the story of the 153 fishes in the final Gospel of the Bible - St John, Chapter 21. This is a story about the third reappearance of Jesus following the resurrection. He appears to several of his disciples on the beach while they are 2000 cubits at sea in a boat, having spent a fruitless night trying to catch fish in nets. The usual exchange occurs, "have you caught anything?", says Jesus. "No!", comes the discouraging reply. Then an unusual response from Jesus, "Cast your nets on the right side of the ship and you'll be fine." The disciples duly do as Jesus says and in no time cannot draw the net into the boat, it is so full of fish. Peter 'drew the net to land full of great fishes, and hundred and fifty and three: yet for all there were, yet was not the net broken.'

The best fishing yarn ever published, it has remained the best known. This text is loaded like the boat, but with an unusual numerical cargo. There are twelve disciples, Jesus was the thirteenth member of the group. There were seven disciples in one boat and they caught nothing, there were five in the second boat and they were able to draw the net in. And then there were 153 fishes. Why that number, why not 231 fishes, or 118 fishes? Well, 153 is the square of 12.369, the number of full moons in the solar year, and it is by applying Pythagoras' theorem in the lunation triangle ($3^2 + 12^2$) that the square root of 153, the longest side or hypotenuse, has to be calculated.

So this story appears to contain much of the numerical detail that is to be found in using the lunation triangle. Additional support comes from the fact that in ancient days the square root of a number was placed within a net rather like a noughts and crosses board, and our modern symbol for a square root looks much like the tool used to mend nets.

This story from the Bible provides strong evidence that the secret of the marriage of sun and moon had been remembered into Christian times. The original wall of the temple at Jerusalem was built as a 5:12 rectangle, and Solomon's Throne is placed on the 3:2 point of the eastern '5' side!

Whether or not this story demonstrates knowledge of this device being continued into the historical period, there is strong evidence that throughout the megalithic cultures of northwestern Europe it was applied exactly as described here. And this is where the story becomes suddenly a lot stranger, meeting a much larger lunation triangle that involves Stonehenge.

The Preseli-Stonehenge Lunation Triangle

During this period of my life I was living in Brittany, France. One day sitting under a sweet chestnut tree, I was idly studying some maps for a forthcoming tour of Stonehenge and Avebury when something just caught my eye. It was Lundy Island, a small dot in the Bristol Channel. It looked as if it was due west of Stonehenge. In addition, directly north of Lundy was the Preseli region. Perhaps you can see where this is going? I thought I'd check this out using the geodetic sums that I had known from teaching navigation and surveying techniques. In the days before internet and Google Earth, it was hard, living in France, to find the latitudes and longitudes of Lundy. Eventually I phoned a friend, and ten minutes later I had the coordinates of the centre of Lundy Island - north 51.178 degrees and west 4.671 degrees. I already knew those for Stonehenge - north 51.178 degrees and 1.8247 degrees. The latitudes were identical - Lundy *centre ville* is *exactly* west of Stonehenge.

I then calculated the distance as 123.4 miles, and, intuiting from the map that the north leg up to Preseli might be '5' to the '12' length from Stonehenge to Lundy, I marked on the map the location that was 51.25 miles north of Lundy. It fell very close to Glandy Cross and the Preseli bluestone site.

So here appeared to be a second and radically different connecting link between the bluestones and Stonehenge, obtained independently from folk

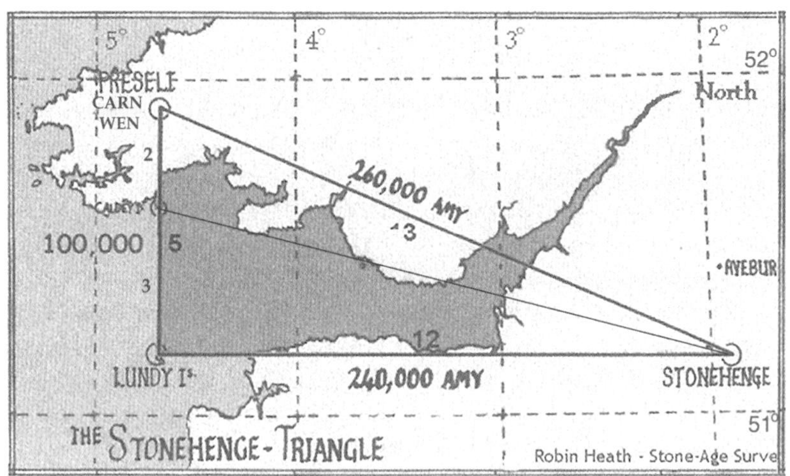

legend or geology. *Stonehenge and the bluestone site form the opposite corners of a huge 5:12 rectangle, accurately so.* This wholly unexpected triangle is shown above.

In the eighteen years since that discovery it has been necessary only to refine the original vision, calculate the distances more precisely and visit the points on the triangle. It is astonishingly accurate.

The 3:2 point falls on the eastern side of Caldey Island, making this a display of geodetic skill that has proved completely unacceptable to any academic disciplines. Google Earth can now inform anyone that the distance from Stonehenge to Lundy central (the '12' side) is 123.4 miles, which is a very little under 240,000 megalithic yards, making this large triangle 2500 times bigger than the one at Stonehenge. It connects astronomically and geometrically to the Preseli bluestone site linked by Herbert Thomas, in the 1920s, to Stonehenge. It has purpose and intent as a statement.

In 2004, I was again looking at a map, and found a further accurate 5:12:13 triangle, this one being 2.5 times larger than the Preseli-Stonhenge triangle. Everybody knows the points on this one, for they are the capital cities of Britain - London, Cardiff and Edinburgh. These points are located in the city centres. Perhaps someone else knows all about this one, but if so they do appear to have kept it secret!

Chapter Seven

Megalithic Wizardry
Well connected monuments

The alignments described in earlier chapters form two types. The first is where an angle has been struck across the landscape to do what lines all do - connect the two places between the ends of the line. Two, three and more locations may also be found 'down the line' to reinforce the reality of the original alignment. It need not involve any reference to the celestial bodies. However, the north-south alignment connecting Pentre Ifan via Llech y Drybedd and across Cardigan Bay to Bardsey is an example where reference has been made to the sky, as the determination of 'north' and 'south' depend on such. This is an example of the second class of alignment, where observation of sun, moon or stars has been implemental in the reason for the alignment's direction and the purpose of built objects placed at its ends.

The lunation triangle falls into this second category because two sides of the triangle are framed to the cardinal points, the '12' side runs east-west, and the '5' side north-west. The extra twist in this cocktail of geodetic expertise is that the objects at the triangle's corners, which, including Caldey Island, provide the 'secret' of marrying the sun and moon together. The cherry in the glass is that the only large built monument within the form is Stonehenge, which means that the form must have been realised prior to the earliest constructions at that location, before 3000 BC.

Stonehenge turns out to be a very well connected monument indeed. It has friends in high places - higher latitudes - and it is to two well known sites that we now turn our attention.

Bryn Celli Ddu & Arbor Low

There is a second example of prehistoric landscape geometry where the three sites that make up the employed geometry are all well known built megalithic monuments. The first is the 'Stonehenge of the North', Arbor Low, near Matlock in the Derbyshire Peak District, the other is Bryn Celli Ddu on Anglesey, in North Wales. Both monuments are found at the same latitude, and are therefore east and west of each other, respectively. Both are very early Neolithic. It turns out that Arbor Low is very close to being due north of Stonehenge. The three sites make a right angle at Arbor Low. It is a simple matter to measure the distances involved and discover the length of the third side - which confirms that these three spectacular megalithic sites define an accurate 3:4:5 triangle. The 3:4:5 geometry is totally familiar within Thom's plans of megalithic monuments, and may be found at scores of megalithic sites - it forms the basis for the perimeter shapes of many non-circular stone rings.

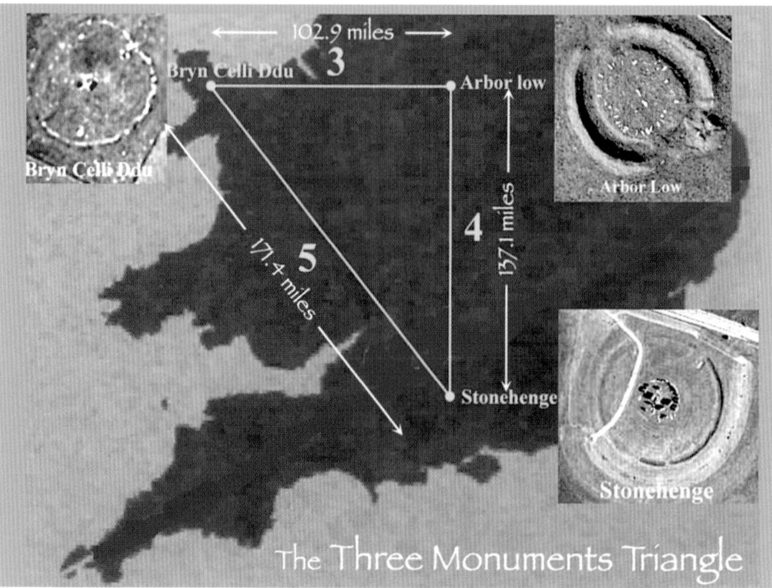

Three major and similar megalithic 'henge' sites accurately linked across the landscape through simple geometry, in this case a 3:4:5 'pythagorean' triangle.

Once the triangle is 'seen', it is then easy to suggest what units of length the builders were applying. It appears to have been 10 Geodetic Units (GU) each of 24/7 miles. This is familiar to those who study ancient metrology as three Royal Miles of 8/7 English miles. The Royal Mile in Edinburgh, from the centre of the Castle to the centre of Holyrood Palace is one Royal mile. The Royal Mile in Edinburgh is exactly what it says it is on the road signs!

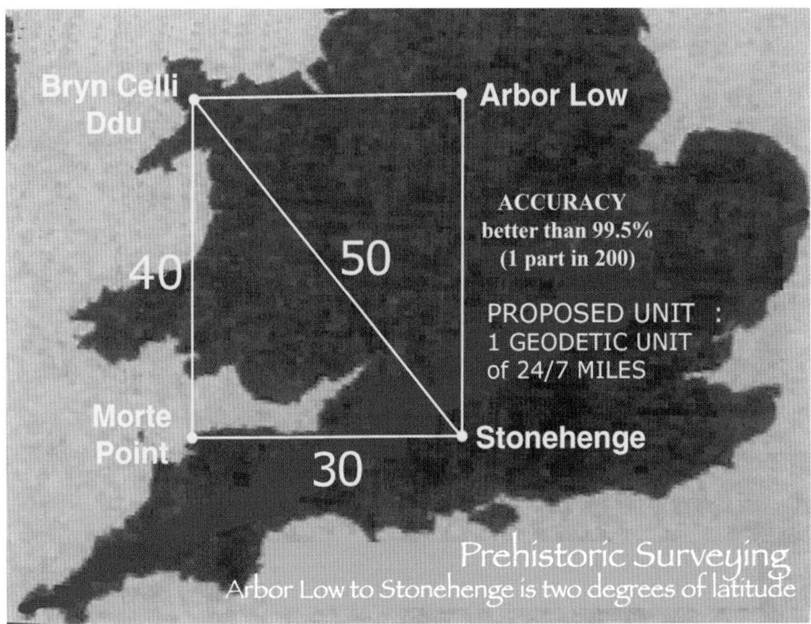

The unit of length employed here is 3 Royal miles, a unit familar within classical metrology, being 8/7 ths of an English mile. The sides of the triangle are 90, 120 and 150 Royal miles, the 3:4:5 relationship is clearly seen. This can easily be checked using Google Earth.

The 3:4:5 triangle is metrologically 30:40:50 GU. It is the more remarkable to discover that these units of length can be directly related to those employed in the Stonehenge-Lundy triangle – whose 5:12:13 proportions are, in the same units, expressed as 15:36:39 GUs. This numerical and metrological link between the two triangles greatly supports the hypothesis that a geodetic grid network was being employed in prehistory. It cannot be a coincidence.

Completing the Rectangle

To complete the implied 4:3 rectangle, it is necessary to define a fourth point directly westwards and at distance '3 units' from Stonehenge. The location is marked by a burial chamber on the headland at Morte Point in North Devon.

A line running westwards from Stonehenge to Morte Point is parallel and coincidental with that providing the base line for the'12' side of the 5:12:13 triangle, from Stonehenge to Lundy. Their lengths are accurately in the ratio of 5:6. The evidence presented here shows once more that orthodox beliefs concerning the prehistoric period in Britain profoundly underestimate the technological expertise and aspirations of the megalith builders.

There are two burial chambers nearby on Mortehoe head, and one of these coincides with the expected position of the fourth corner to high accuracy. The southern one has an identical latitude to Stonehenge and a longitude of 4° 12' 07". While not a well-known site and ruinous, it is nevertheless man-made, prehistoric and correctly located to provide the fourth 'corner' of the rectangle.

The three principal sites that define this form began their life very early in the era of henge building, during the Neolithic. All three sites retain their clearly visible henge structure and all have been dated prior to 3000 BC. Recent work undertaken by archaeologists at Bryn Celli Ddu suggests that its henge may date from as early as 4500 BC, and material discovered in the eponymous car park postholes at Stonehenge has been radiocarbon dated to earlier that 4000 BC, possibly 6000 BC.

Arbor Low is a name thought by Aubrey Burl to be derived from *eordburgh hlaw*, Saxon for 'earthwork mound'. Burl writes, 'Probably a late Neolithic monument of around 3000 BC. The NE facing cove may have been aligned to the major northern moonrise'. Burl suggests that it may have been the 'very first structure here'. Arbor Low 'lies at the heart of a landscape of eight Early Neolithic chambered tombs including Five Wells, Brushfield and Harborough Rocks. In turn it became the centre of dozens of Bronze Age cairns. It is one of the wonders of megalithic Britain.'

Of the Bryn Celli Ddu site, Burl writes that this site '*cannot be omitted from any guide book about stone circles*'. He refers to the original site as a 'circle-henge', the stone ellipse (19.2m x 17.4m) erected on the henge was destroyed by Late Neolithic passage tomb builders over 4000 years ago. 'The ellipse was wrecked by the tomb builders. Five stones were removed, one buried, others toppled and smashed with heavy blocks. The two largest stones (which remain) had stood at the north and south. By the south stone (7' long) were fragments of quartz, By the north pillar, 8' long, was the cremation of an 8 - 10 year old girl, a partial cremation of another girl lay by the western stone. Emphasis upon cardinal points was common in early stone circles'.

Burl leaves his readers in no doubt as to the importance of Arbor Low and Bryn Cell Ddu. Both monuments are visited by thousands of visitors a year wishing to connect to a mysterious past that has been largely forgotten.

Bryn Celli Ddu
Archaeological reconstruction of original monument

The earliest monument at Bryn Celli Ddu was a ditch and bank surrounding a flat elliptical henge. A stone circle was built on the henge with up to sixteen stones. This structure was later destroyed by a change in the culture, and a stone-lined passage grave was built and later covered in a large mound of earth. This fine and later monument is shown overleaf.

Astronomy, Geometry & Geography Coincide

It was first noted in 1908 that the passage angle at Bryn Celli Ddu was aligned to the midsummer sunrise. Sir Norman Lockyer undertook the first accurate survey of the monument to include astronomical assessment of the site, and in 2004, I repeated this work and published the initial results. The passage angle was determined by theodolite, to be an azimuth of 53° 07'. Outside the chamber there is a radial row of stones (*shown on the photograph opposite*), the extreme left-hand stone can be seen at the bottom of the middle leg of the theodolite in the photograph on the left. This stone was discovered to mark the axis.

The raised horizon altitude visible from the end of the passage was measured and the midsummer sunrise in 3000 BC was calculated to be an azimuth of 53° 04'. While the passage angle may have been tampered with during restorations of this site, the horizon altitude leading to the azimuth calculation for midsummer sunrise cannot have been. Both the measured angle of the passage and the azimuth of the midsummer sunrise at Bryn Celli Ddu during the epoch when the burial chamber was constructed coincide extremely closely with the latitude of the site (53° 12'). This same angle also happens to be one of the angles of a 3:4:5 triangle! *What* is going on here?

This angle is seen to occur in several independent ways:- 1. It is the latitude of its location 2. It is the orientation of the passage into the central area. 3. It is the azimuth angle of the midsummer sunrise. 4. It is inherent in the 3:4:5 triangle geometry from Stonehenge. Were all these things incorporated by the builders? If so, then they represented a very skilled culture.

If these things were intentional, as evidence now suggests they were, then the aspirations, capabilities and subtle intent incorporated in these monuments are truly astonishing and suggest that the neolithic period in Britain included a skill base which until now has been totally unrecognised.

BRYN CELLI DDU
Latitude of Site =53° 12′ 26″N
Angle of Passage =53° 04′ 55″
Sunrise angle =53° 04′ 55″
Angle of 3-4-5 to Stonehenge =53° 07′ 48″

Bryn Celli Ddu, Anglesey

Two 'Arthur' Alignments

There are two spin-off alignments from these two huge landscape triangles that are worth visiting, because both pass through the Preseli region and each substantiates the reality of the two large triangles generated from Stonehenge. They are also associated with the Welsh word 'arth' meaning Bear, or the name 'Arthur'. The legend of Arthur and the Knights of the Round Table has remained extremely popular since the Romances, written during the chivalric age of crusades, courtly love and knightly virtue.

The name Arthur can be translated as Great Bear, *Arth Fawr*, and may identify our 'Once and Future King' as being named after a much older polar myth. The spinning of the earth on its axis has given birth to so many myths relating to death and resurrection that it would be impossible to list them all here, and the subject has been well covered in academic and popular books alike. What is of concern here is that the need to find True North is imperative in any act of surveying, mapping or understanding direction, at sea or on land. For some years I have been engaged in a project that has looked for the evidence linking alignments, and particularly though not exclusively north-south alignments, with place names or legends about Bears, King Arthur or the root word 'arth'.

The Great Bear is the constellation we use today to determine True North and it appears to have been used for this purpose as far back as we have records. It is the obvious choice. While the pole star changes every once in a while, or takes a 'gap millennium' every now and then, the Great Bear's haunches always point to the axis, and that is and always has been north of an observer located in the northern hemisphere of the earth.

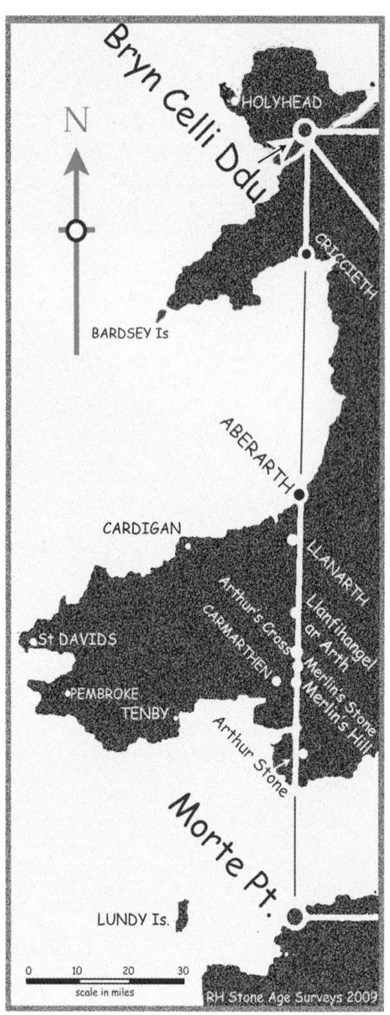

Two alignments are of great interest in this regard. The first is the north-south line that defines the Welsh side of the 3:4 rectangle connecting Stonehenge to Bryn Celli ddu. This line supports the polar nature of the Arthurian mythos and it equally supports the 3:4 rectangle by providing along its passage through West Wales an unexpectedly large number of Arthur, 'arth' and Merlin related places and legends. It is the oddness of this occurring that first drew me to undertake a thorough inspection of the old maps and walk much of the landscape to obtain a feel for what was going on. The result was both convincing of the theory of polar relatedness and confirming of an ancient practice of naming prehistoric alignments that run north-south 'Arthur'. This practice appears to have continued into the late Middle Ages before finally running out of steam.

The map on the left shows the alignment between Morte Point and Bryn Celli Ddu, with some of the larger and more significant town names marked out along the way. The table below elaborates on these and provides geodetic data to indicate how narrow is this corridor of name and legend-related places that cuts through the right hand side of the Preseli region.

SITE	LATITUDE (N)	LONGITUDE (W)	ERROR (FROM MEAN)
Bryn Celli Ddu	53° 12′ 27″	4° 14′ 05″	+ 7.5″
Criccieth Castle	52° 54′ 50″	4° 13′ 50″	- 5.5″
Aberarth	52° 14′ 54″	4° 14′ 07″	+ 9.5″
Llandewi Ch., Aberarth	52° 14′ 50″	4° 13′ 52″	- 5.5″
Llanarth (Parish Town)	52° 11′ 50″	4° 18′ 24″	+ 4′ 27″
Llanfihangel ar Arth	52°02′ 10″	4° 15′ 00″	+ 1′ 03″
Arthur's Cross	51° 54′ 34″	4° 13′ 38″	- 19.4″
Merlin's Stone, Abergwili	51° 52′ 16″	4° 14′ 30″	+ 32.5″
Merlin's Hill, Abergwili	51° 52′ 14″	4° 14′ 30″	+ 32.5″
Aberarthne	51° 51′ 40″	4° 08′ 10″	- 5′ 57″
CARMARTHEN (County Town)	51° 51′ 37″	4° 18′ 11″	+ 4′ 14″
Arthur Stone, Gower	51° 36′ 43″	4° 11′ 20″	- 2′ 37″
Burial Chamber, Morte Point	51° 10′ 42″	4° 11′ 30″	- 2′ 27″
Morte Point	51° 11′ 20″	4° 14′ 20″	+ 22.5″

Total length of alignment is 140 miles

Azimuth (bearing) of alignment from Morte Point to Bryn Celli Ddu is 0 4′ 20″

The Mean longitude is 4 13′ 57″ (14 sites)

Average second of longitude = 62 feet (19m)

Stone Age Surveys 2009

The Preseli Arthur Alignment

The second alignment relates to the 5:12:13 Stonehenge-Preseli triangle, and it too suggests knowledge of the triangle continued until well into the early Middle Ages. This alignment does not run north-south, it runs north-west to south-east as the 'quarter-cut' or diagonal of a square, one of whose sides is the northern leg of the giant triangle from Lundy to the Preseli bluestone outcrop. This diagonal terminates at Dunster, a town steeped in the Arthurian story, through a legend connecting the town with St. Caranog, a sixth century holy man who converted much of central Cornwall to the Celtic Christian faith.

Originally from Wales, and having founded a church at Llangrannog on the Cardiganshire coast, directly north of St Clears, Caranog had constructed a floating altar, which he launched onto the waters of the Bristol Channel, vowing to preach wherever it came to land. The altar arrived at Dunster, where Arthur lived. At that time, Arthur was looking for a huge dragon that was terrorising the inhabitants of nearby Carhampton. Caranog inquired where his altar was and Arthur told the saint that he knew its location and, if the saint would only slay the dragon, he could have his altar. The saint kept his side of the bargain, and Arthur duly produced the altar, saying that he had been trying to use it as a table, but that everything he had placed on it kept sliding off.

Whatever the meaning of this legend once was, it is today as remote as the megaliths. All it tells us is the location (place), that Arthur (surveying or navigation) was involved and that a dragon was causing trouble. The Church had no truck with dragons, they were a representation of the energy of the earth and hence of paganism, which is why so many latterday depictions of St Michael and St George frequently show these holy men spearing dragons.

The first step in this kind of work is to place a transparent ruler on the map, from Dunster to the Preseli bluestone outcrop at Carn Meini. Geodetic sums show that it lies at forty-five degrees east of north. The next step is to note the places on the route. The alignment crosses the Gower coast, passes the Arthur Stone, crosses the Kidwelly estuary to Warley Point, St Anthony's well near the fine castle at Llansteffan. The line is taking the eye through Norman territory, Templar hot-spots and along a well-attested Pilgrimage route. Along the Taf estuary, the alignment passes through the ruined but utterly magical St Michael church at Llandeilo Abercowin, next to Pilgrim's Rest and part of the Treventy estate, and continues on to the castle mound and St Mary church in St Clears. Opposite the church is a fine old customs

The splendidly ruinous St Michael church on the Taf estuary at Trefenty farm, St Clears, lies on a line drawn between Dunster and the Preseli outcrops. Norman noblemen's graves (right)are particularly wonderful and the magical location remains a pilgrimage destination to this day.

house with a wall plaque depicting a boar. After St Clears, another very remote church is passed near Grove Farm, then a 'camp' just south of Llanboidy, and near a burial chamber and standing stones at Cross Hands.

The alignment then crosses the Taf, heading for the summit of Carn Wen and the little town of Mynachlog-ddu (Black Monastery), where it enters an altogether more prehistoric phase and passes over three 'Arthur' sites in as many miles. Carn Arthur and Bedd Arthur are sited within a third of a mile from the bluestone outcrop, while the third site, Eisteddfa Arthur (Arthur's seat') is a bluestone standing stone in the private back garden of a farm estate just north of Brynberian.

Eisteddfa Arthur - Arthur's Seat, Brynberian, Preseli

The legend goes that Arthur sat here and watched his men fighting the 'stinking boar', Twrch Trwych from here during the Battle of Cwmcerwyn. It is true that this stone indeed offers a level of comfort not normally found with standing stones! Following the alignment on, it passes over the 'fort' in Tycanol woods, an 'interesting' place where you need to be clear and know your own motives, then between Pentre Ifan and the outcrops of Carn Meibion Owen where it then meets a fine standing bluestone in a field just above the A487 road at Pont Clydach (*below*). Across the road and the alignment passes adjacent to a 'settlement' and then joins Newport Golf Club, where there are two rather fine quartz standing stones, unmarked on the map and which may be recent. The line terminates on a wonderful and wild stretch of beach, with caves and waterfalls under the cliffs, and touches the conspicuous navigational marker rock of carregydrywy, 'rock of the wren'.

Clydach stone

Large sections of this alignment are walkable, and take you through varied landscapes which are always beautiful and where you will always learn a great deal about the past.

The alignment draws attention to a medieval anomaly that raises the eyebrows of anyone who hears of it. The Stonehenge Preseli triangle seems to have a reflection of itself drawn across the landscape of Somerset, Devon and Cornwall, and this alignment through the Preselis and its reflection reflect identical town names either side of the Bristol Channel. Apart from supporting a belief that the Celtic Church and the later Normans knew all about these geodetic pathways, it solidly upholds the reality of the prehistoric triangle.

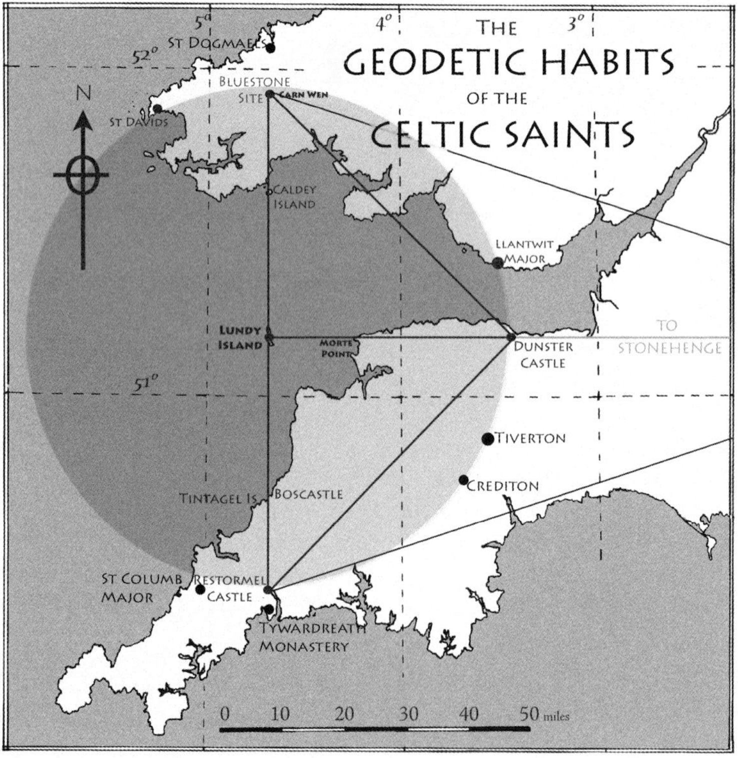

Extensions to the northern axis pass through Mynachlog-ddu and St Dogmaels, where the Normans built a grand Abbey on the earlier Celtic Church site. The southern axis passes through Tywardreath in Cornwall where a large Benedictine priory was built following the Norman conquest.

At Old Cleeve, near Dunster, one of the largest medieval monasteries in Southern England, the Cistercians built Cleeve Abbey.

On a more secular level, the following diagram may make you smile about the nature of town 'twinning' and naming in times gone by. Same names, each pair running north-south of each other and equidistant from the Stonehenge to Lundy line. One couldn't make this stuff up, and it beats *The Da Vinci Code* into a cocked hat- it's not fiction and it's home grown.

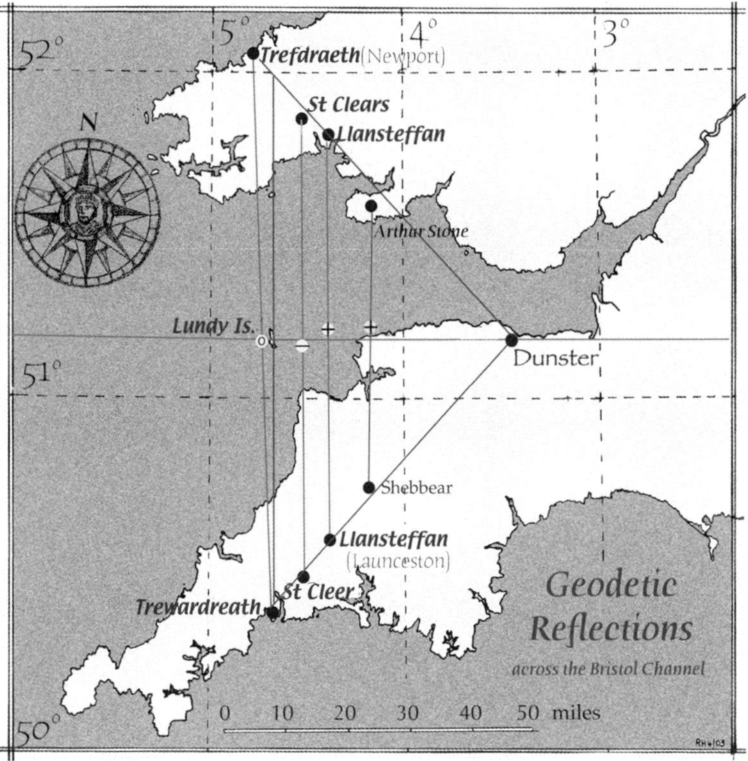

With this display of geodetic pyrotechnics we leave the larger landscape for a final investigation into prehistoric motivations within the Preseli hills, returning to Newport (Trefdraeth), whose name is identical to that of Tywardreath in Cornwall - *Town on the Beach*. They are aligned north-south.

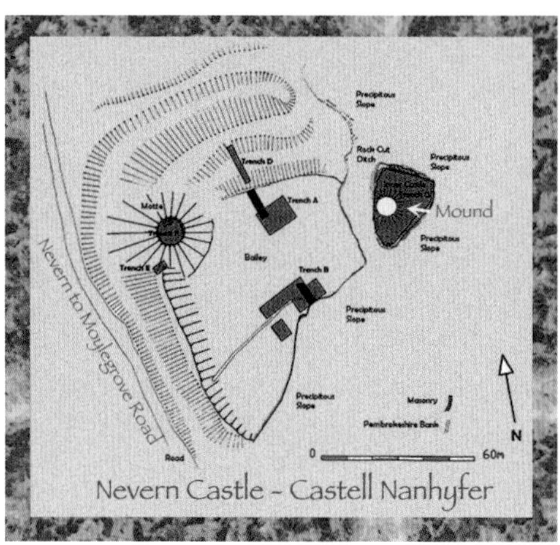

Nevern Castle is one of the most beautiful locations in the Preseli region, a peaceful place ideally suited to a picnic with friends or a little solitude amongst the Beech trees, the bird song and wildflowers. It is an unbelievable commanding site, skirted by precipitous gorges to the east and south, and a few hundred feet due north of Nevern church, with its 'bleeding' yew, massive carved stone megalith with cross on top and filled with objects of huge historical interest. Many people find that they connect to some force or energy at this location, and for whatever reasons, this site has drawn Christians and wise folk ever since the earliest Celtic saints. The church is dedicated to St Brynach, of Carningli angel fame. It is a 'must visit' location.

Chapter Eight

The Preseli Vesica

There was an old woman
Lived under a hill.
And if she's not gone
She lives there still.

Traditional Nursery Rhyme

One might suppose that for a culture that meticulously studied the sun and moon, the luminaries would become gods, and the alignments described previously would be thought sacred, temples to a higher Power. Some proof that this was the case can be found from Roman and very early medieval records. Pope Gregory, who occupied the Papal seat contemporaneously with St David, described the British as a nation,

> '*placed in an obscure corner of the world ...hitherto ... wholly taken up with the adoration of wood and stones*'.

Pope Gregory the Great then issued an edict that Christian churches were to be built on the newly destroyed sites of the pagan monuments.

An earlier and rather different type of conqueror, Julius Caesar wrote of the Druids that,

> '*..they have many discussions concerning the Sun, Moon and stars and their movements.. and the strength and powers of the immortal gods*'

These two quotes from independent sources tell us that the sun, the moon, wood and stones were the traditionally 'adored' (worshipped) objects of interest within ancient paganism. They were sacred. Three of the items from this list are virtually immortal, while the fourth, wood, has long since disintegrated into the wet landscape of West Wales. The combination of geometry and astronomy integrates all the three surviving items on this list - sun, moon and stone - into something that belongs in the category of being Sacred Geometry.

Sacred Geometry is one of those subjects where logic combines with mysticism. Music (harmony) and astrology are two others. These subjects meld intellect and emotion and do fit comfortably into the modern rationally-based world. But Sacred Geometry is, and always has been, the flagship discipline for understanding universal existence and it remains the prime entry point for dialogue between human and Divine existence, between temporal and eternal. On the door of Plato's academy it read 'No one enters here unless they know geometry.' Through observing the forms and nature of the physical world, reckoning with the measurements and understanding nature's patterns through number and geometrical techniques, our ancestors could and did receive symbolic messages from the Gods, and were thereby enabled to embrace a cosmology of Divine Order.

In earlier chapters it was made clear that the prehistoric sun and moon watchers in Preseli had become aware of geometric order in the skies, this being reflected in the orientation and choice of location for many of their most impressive sites providing affirmation of this. The Preseli-Stonehenge triangle demonstrates this cosmic understanding being manifested on the landscape. The Stonehenge - Arbor Low - Bryn Celli Ddu triangle suggests something rather different - surveying and geodetic knowledge evidenced as geometrical patterns on the landscape. Here is a third and spectacular example of this activity in the Preselis, at Newport.

Returning to Pentre Ifan

There is a feature on the summit of Carningli that lies directly west of Pentre Ifan, and I often use this west-point as the reference object for the theodolite, setting the instrument to read 270 degrees when the crosswires are on this point. Once I swung the instrument clockwise to demonstrate the bearing of Coetan Arthur and the northern position of Llech y Drybedd and in so doing I caught a glimpse of the Norman church tower at Nevern. The angle of the tower was almost exactly thirty degrees west of north.

Another time I was sitting on Carningli summit, and looked across to Nevern church tower. Almost invisible in the tree cover, the angle was around 30 degrees, or thirty degrees east of north. I made a mental note to look at the relationship between Pentre Ifan, Nevern church and Carningli peak once I had returned home to my maps and large drawing board. Why would this be of interest? Because Nevern church is located so that the angles to both Pentre Ifan and Carningli appeared to add to sixty degrees, and Pentre Ifan and Carningli lie on an East-West line. The three locations appeared to form an equilateral (equal sided) triangle.

Upon returning home I took out the map and laid it out it across my big drawing board. There was indeed an equilateral triangle, but the apex was not Nevern church but a few hundred feet to the north, at Nevern castle. The apex of an equilateral triangle from Carn Ingli and Pentre Ifan was located on the 'faery' mound on the eastern side of the monument, a well known site that people visit to find replenishment.

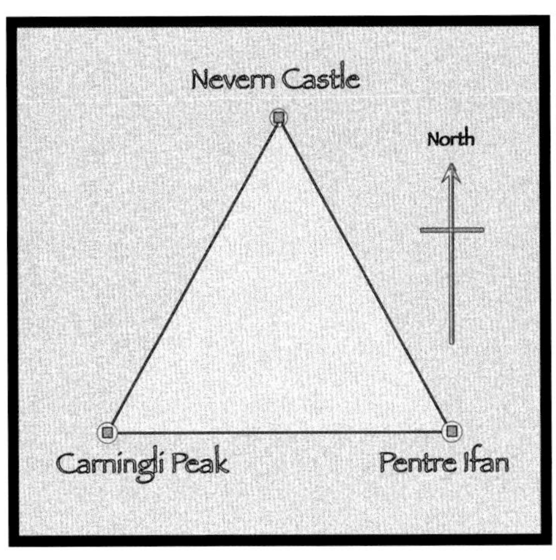

I checked this using Google Earth, and confirmed my findings. Astonished, I revisited each of the sites involved and retook their GPS coordinates. This confirmed that these three sites were located to form an accurate equilateral triangle. The mound at Nevern castle is the northern point, Pentre Ifan the eastern point, and the (allegedly) Bronze Age fort, more specifically a platform just below the summit of Carningli, provides the western point, the illustration above showing both the shape and scale of this triangle. The triangle is astonishingly accurate, and this places Pentre Ifan, Nevern castle and Carningli peak into a geometrical relationship that cannot be accidental. Two of these sites - Nevern castle and Carningli are man-made additions to already striking natural landscape features, while the third site, Pentre Ifan, is wholly man-made. This is Neolithic Sacred Geometry at its best, a profoundly significant message left on the landscape from before 3500 BC.

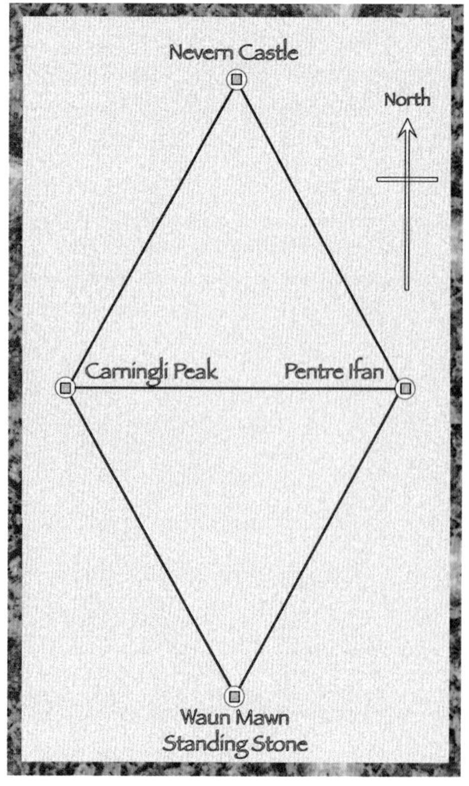

Students of the Traditional Arts know that the equilateral triangle is the basis for the *vesica piscis*. Within the intersecting circles of a *vesica piscis* are two equilateral triangles arranged back to back, to form a diamond shape. The obvious next question was to now ask: *Is there a second triangle south of the 'Nevern Triangle'?*

It did not take long to confirm that there was a standing stone that completed the second equilateral triangle. Waun Mawn is a six foot high single stone within a rising escarpement on the southern side of Cnwc yr Hydd, whose location matches perfectly the requirements for the apex of a second triangle. These two triangles together form the basis of a *vesica piscis*. Waun Mawn has already been described, with photos on page 4 (*top right*), page 64 (*top left*) and page 158 (*bottom left*) The stone lies directly south of the castle mound: the two identical triangles are arranged such that their axis of symmetry aligns north-south, while their shared sides align east-west. The cardinal points of the compass have been accurately defined.

The chances of this geometric arrangement coming about by coincidence are almost nothing, that it is also oriented to the four cardinal points makes that likelihood the square root of almost nothing. No rational person should baulk at my suggestion that this forms a man-made structure deliberately and accurately placed on the landscape. It is an expression of landscape art conceived of by Stone Age people who well understood geometry and astronomy and evidently possessed the practical surveying skills to implement their intended design on the landscape. This realisation begs an important question: *why would they have done such a thing?*

Several interesting sequels followed this discovery, and these further validated the structure. Firstly, the distance between each link of the triangles - the length of their sides - was carefully measured using GPS and Google Earth. Secondly, the distance from Nevern mound to Llech y Drybedd turned out to be a similar length to all the other five side-lengths of the two interlocked triangles. Thirdly, from the Nevern mound, the bearing angle to Llech y Drybedd is sixty degrees east of north. It is therefore clearly an extension of the triangle side that runs from Carningli to Nevern castle mound, and significantly increases the probability that the two triangles were a planned man-made activity. The table below reveals an remarkably narrow spread of lengths - all six within 99.4% of the average distance.

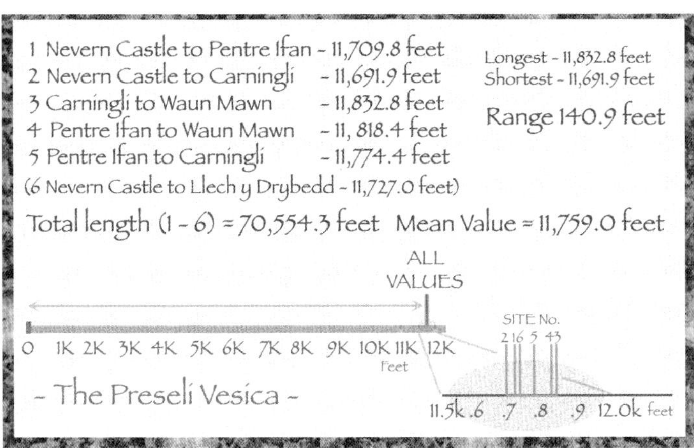

1 Nevern Castle to Pentre Ifan	- 11,709.8 feet
2 Nevern Castle to Carningli	- 11,691.9 feet
3 Carningli to Waun Mawn	- 11,832.8 feet
4 Pentre Ifan to Waun Mawn	- 11, 818.4 feet
5 Pentre Ifan to Carningli	- 11,774.4 feet
(6 Nevern Castle to Llech y Drybedd	- 11,727.0 feet)

Longest - 11,832.8 feet
Shortest - 11,691.9 feet
Range 140.9 feet

Total length (1 - 6) = 70,554.3 feet Mean Value = 11,759.0 feet

- The Preseli Vesica -

Table showing the analysis of the variations in side lengths of the two triangles. Llech y Drybedd, which is located at the same distance and the correct angle as to form an extension of the construction, greatly proves the case that this structure was accurately built with intent.

Having found the triangles, and possibly part of what may have been a third triangle, it was time to draw out the *vesica piscis* on the landscape around them in order to ascertain whether these two equilateral triangles were indeed part of a *vesica (opposite)*. There is ample reason for believing in prehistoric origins for this shape, the burial cairn on Foel Feddau summit is *vesica* shaped. The *vesica piscis* is perhaps the principle symbol of the Christian faith, its geometry found in church windows and in Christian iconography. A huge example supports the roof structure of Wells Cathedral. The fish symbol seen on the rear windows of cars is an emaciated version of the formal geometry of the *vesica*.

The head of the *vesica piscis* lies at Nevern castle. Underneath the precipitous drop that surrounds the south side of the castle there was once a large and most significant early Christian monastic settlement which grew up adjacent to the spot where Nevern church now stands. The Pilgrim's Cross alongside the path leading south from the church provides an indication of the importance of the location during the early Christian period. Irish occupation from the fifth to the eleventh century has literally added its mark in the form of Ogham stones, one of which is set into a window sill, while the design of a

The four sites whose location suggests the geometry of a vesica piscis was laid out on the Preseli landscape in prehistoric times. The diagram opposite shows how these sites define the geometry.

second inscribed stone set in the adjacent sill is pre-Norman and probably early Celtic Christian Church of 'Irish influence'. The magnificent thirteen foot carved bluestone cross which stands adjacent to the south wall of the church may be inscribed in Viking style and is probably the best example of this kind of inscribed standing stone in Wales (*see page 31*). The separate Christianized top section and the carvings are perhaps a later addition to what was once a very large bluestone megalith. And where might that have come from? Some local historians think that the stone was once placed up the hill at the castle, in prehistoric times, and a suitably large stone hole was indeed revealed at the recent archaeological 'dig' undertaken in 2009 by Dr Chris Caple from Durham University. The true origin of the stone may, of course, be from the bluestone outcrop.

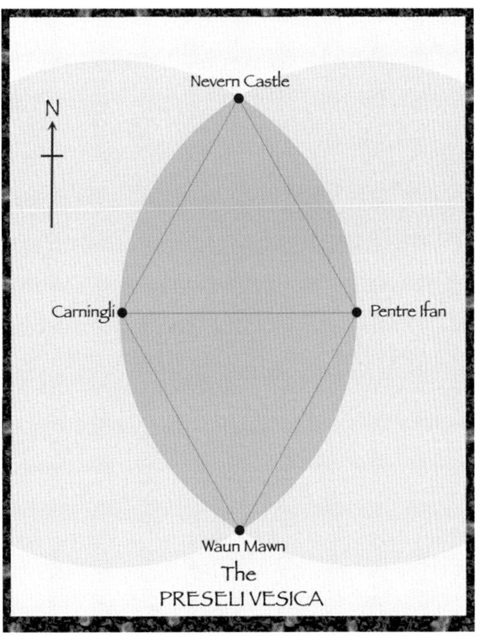

The present Nevern church sports a Norman tower and internally is now a typical example of Victorian renovation. Beneath the calvanistic starkness, the church's foundations rest on a location of utter sanctity and this can and does connect visitors to a tangible sense of peace. The recent 'dig' above the church has affected this atmosphere markedly, and destruction to tree cover and other invasive work at the castle, while lawful, has regrettably taken a large toll on the site, from which it will take years to recover. The two photographs of a 'protest picnic' and circle dance at the mound are shown heading this chapter and at the top of the page opposite. Visitors to the mound may find the spot a very different place as the archaeological work progresses.

The View from the Mound

At the mound looking to the south-west there is a fine view of the sacred mountain that holds the whole area together - Carningli. Once the leaves have fallen from the beech and oak trees that surround what locals call the 'faery mound', much more is revealed. It is possible to view, to the south-east, the Preseli bluestone site and much of 'Preseli Top' (from Foel Drygarn to Foel Feddau and Cwmcerwyn). The outcrops of Carn Meibion Owen are visible and, if one looks hard enough in the right direction, Pentre Ifan itself. The viewing window more or less encompasses the entire sixty degree angle of the northernmost equilateral triangle defining the geometry of the *vesica piscis*. The 'faery mound' is perfectly co-ordinated into the inherent geometry of the local landscape. This function has nothing to do with medieval castle builders, it is clearly prehistoric in origin.

Where does all this lead? All the sites defining the triangles are major sites, two are widely displayed on tourist literature throughout the area and beyond - the modern symbols of the entire region. People travel from all over the world to see Pentre Ifan, and Carningli in particular has, during the past half century, restored its earlier status as a place of spiritual importance and pilgrimage. But why and who are these modern pilgrims?

The Good Life in West Wales

The 'hippy' revolution of the 60s may be a curious start to providing an answer to the question of why there is a *vesica piscis* arrayed across the landscape here. But probing beneath the surface of social patterns and changes that have taken place here in Preseli are seen to connect these things with that geometrical structure from the Stone Age. Although the modern world still associates the *vesica piscis* form with Christianity, it derives from much earlier cultural roots and a much older symbolism.

The *vesica* was known about long before the Age of Pisces that began our modern era. It may be found on bone-dry Egyptian Heiroglyphics and, now, it has been found laid out on the wet soil of Pembrokeshire's National Park. The numerical and geometrical truths that lay behind this symbol are far more exciting than that revealed in recent films based on semi-fictional novels. The *vesica* shape is a *generative* force, it brings things forth.

One trouble with the modern world is that people think that symbols are merely shapes, without being aware of the effects they invoke. For example, the *logos* of mind-numbing advertising promotions. The pentagon star has become the name of the world's largest military centre, and the *logo* symbol for Texaco or a soft drink company, or expensive trainers. For most of mankind's past, such symbols, steeped in sacred geometry held a power that was associated with its shape. The pentagon was associated with magical power, as was the recently shamed swastika, while the *vesica piscis* was associated with Creation itself, as a God-Goddess, Father-Mother relationship, with humankind or the planet as the Mabon or Holy Child.

The two intersecting circles that form the construction of the vesica form what the Italians call *Mandorla*, the almond, the shape that resembles the female generative organ and from which all human life emerges into the material world. The *vesica* is therefore primarily a symbol of the Divine Feminine, the Goddess from which all new life springs. In a word - *Birth.*

During the past fifty years those seeking an alternative lifestyle initiated a social revolution. In this region two major advantages made that entirely possible. One was very affordable housing with land attached, the other was the natural beauty of the region. People came here in droves. As time went on a third advantage emerged, the area accumulated like-minded souls to provide outlets for alternative cultural activities and community living.

This kind of material may appear strange to a reader who has just purchased or borrowed this book expecting a traditional treatment about bluestone megaliths in West Wales. But the truth of the matter is that several of these megalithic sites have been placed to form a *vesica piscis* and that shape changes consciousness - *especially if you are living inside it.*

Sacred Geometry - A Metaphysical Component

Sacred Geometry was traditionally thought to provide an intermediary process between the Divine consciousness and the physical world, Nowhere was that process better represented than in the geometry of the *Vesica Piscis.*

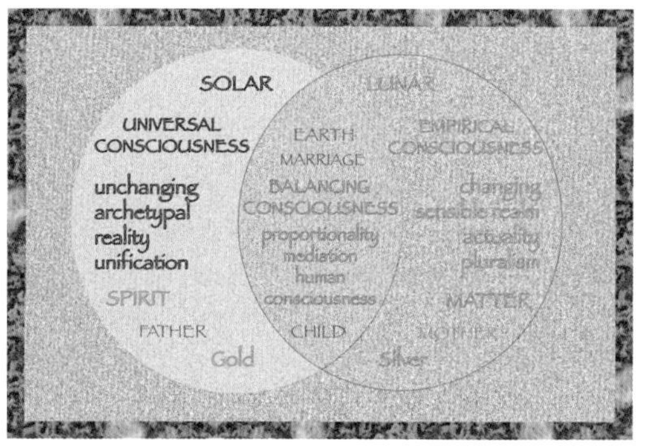

This form - a prime symbol for reconciling polarity - is the intersection of the two circles, and represents the middle ground between male and female, light and dark, left and right, and between God and man. In this last role it represents a link between universal consciousness and the 'fluctuating actuality of empirical consciousness'. In order to play a role in this linkage, human consciousness must partake of both. As such, it must blend both male and female, the Father-Mother qualities, in equal measure. It remains hampered in finding this balance between apparent opposites because, in the modern world the male principle remains dominant and the subjects of mathematics and geometry, traditionally associated with the feminine principle, have become shackled to predominantly masculine approaches to mathematical and geometrical activity. These include the design of oxymoronical 'better' weapons and the need to conquer countries, economies and markets.

It follows that if one discovers a *vesica piscis* on the landscape it immediately indicates a very important location or space from where to observe and discover the birth of new ideas. A repeated renewal of alternative and creative ideas is likely to emerge. Sacred Geometry traditionally involved working either in a meditational way with these shapes, or in studying their geometry, or both. But however one takes in the energy of a fundamental geometrical symbol the outcome is likely to be that inner changes will be set in motion that awaken the dormant aspects of one's consciousness, currently termed the personal unconscious.

By actually living inside a geometry like the *vesica*, one has already taken the first steps to separate from the collective unconscious, which is currently engaged in taking humanity down a new path, unknown to previous cultures, where God no longer exists and where the universe is a chaotic place.

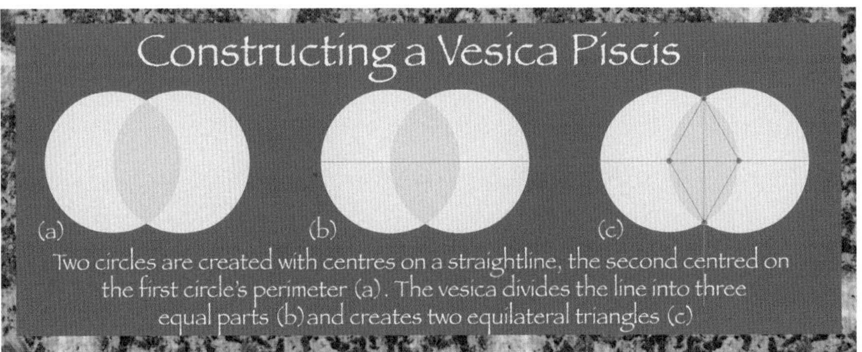

Constructing a Vesica Piscis
(a)
(b)
(c)
Two circles are created with centres on a straightline, the second centred on the first circle's perimeter (a). The vesica divides the line into three equal parts (b) and creates two equilateral triangles (c)

The Pattern of the Past

This book has shown that long before the present structure at Stonehenge was erected, the people who lived in the Bluestone region had developed sufficiently accurate skills in astronomy and geometry to then have possessed the capabilities needed to build Stonehenge, a thousand years later. They were clearly implementing these skills within some kind of cultural system about which we previously knew virtually nothing and which was at least on a par with the achievements of the Wessex culture. In laying out *vesicas* on their landscape (the Foel Feddau cairn is the second example) it has to be considered that the Preseli culture was aware of the potency of the symbols they were employing. These were intensely creative people!

One might have thought that all those antiquarians and archaeologists over the centuries would have had the curiousity to investigate if any of the wonderful megalithic structures found here were connected in some way with their neighbours. Nothing! And since Herbert Thomas's paper in 1923, one might have thought that more people might have asked the obvious question: *why were the Preseli bluestones so important to the earlier constructions at Stonehenge?* Only in the past twenty years has that question been addressed. In the popular press and media, the answer has been seen to be little more than a reissue of Geoffrey's fable about Merlin and the healing stones, where Stonehenge becomes a hospital A&E department. Answers found elsewhere in this book run a little deeper that this, but remain unreported at large.

But anyone who has enjoyed a well-lived lifetime in these parts would have figured out from the history of the Nevern and Newport area that movers and shakers arrive and live here and that, particularly during the past 50 years, something rather unusual has been going on.

The Alternative Movement in Preseli

If one considers that the *vesica piscis* is a generator of new cultural ideas, then finding one placed in the Preseli landscape offers some pretty convincing confirmation. The alternative culture began here in the 60s, when the acknowledged father of the self-sufficiency movement moved here from Suffolk, with his wife Sally and young family. John Seymour was a visionary, a true radical traditionalist, and he came to live practically under the brooding shadow of Carningli, buying the farm Fachongle Isaf, in Cilgwyn, near Newport. His family still live nearby. In his farmyard, unknown to him, lay the very central point of the *vesica piscis*. The recent erection of a large fallen bluestone on the exact location was undertaken without any knowledge of its significance in the *vesica*.

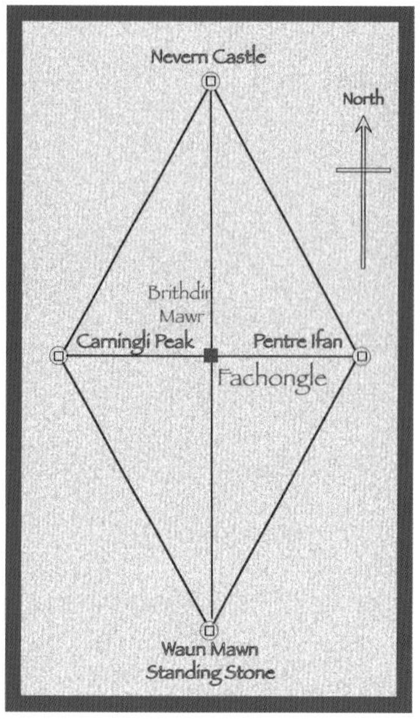

John's output of books, magazine articles, radio and television programmes influenced all who followed the 'back to nature' reaction to post-war industrialisation and uncertainty. This movement spawned one of the most succesful sit-coms, *The Good Life*, which introduced everyone to the issues connected with environmental etiquette in a popular and light-hearted way.

Not that John was ever light-hearted about the way the world was going, he exposed scandal after scandal in multinational companies, governments and the food supply industry. Like a latter day William Cobbett, John was right at the centre of all of these things, and was soon to be joined by Satish Kumar, who lived just a stone's throw from John and who set up the journal *Resurgence* and played a seminal role in the creation of alternative 'Human Scale' educational techniques, eventually founding The Little School in Hartland, Devon. He played a major role in the anti-nuclear movement and in the Peace Movement. Satish, very aptly for this book, talks a great deal about the spiritual compass, and the spirituality of Nature.

After John Seymour moved to Fachongle Isaf, thousands of other people read his books, absorbed his philosophy and came in search of this new energy that John and Satish were describing. Thousands of New Age folk moved to West Wales and many of these settled near Newport. In the 90s, Chris Day, a renown 'Steiner' architect and author of *Places of the Soul* lived at Fachongle. His innovative and beautiful buildings now pepper the Preseli region. A Steiner school was set up here at Nant y Cwm.

Today the place is a thriving community of environmentally friendly folk, their homes powered from their own windmill, and growing much of their own food supply and making a mature statement concerning the kind of world they want to see for their own children and grandchildren. Just a few hundred yards to the northwest of Fachongle another community, Brithdir Mawr, sprang up during the 1990s, and also sports a large windmill and a viable community of dedicated ecologically sound members.

A walk down the farm track through the farmyard at Brithdir Mawr leads down into a large wood almost on the north-south axis of the *vesica piscis* where, during the mid 90s, a major player in the alternative housing movement built what has probably become the most famous sustainable house in the country. Tony Wrench and his wife Faith built their sustainable roundhouse from little more than tree trunks, branches, turf, clay, hard work and love. The house is almost invisible until you stand within a few yards of it. Many universities have conducted experiments in the house on energy consumption and other domestic matters relating to sustainable living. Their statistics paved the way for a new understanding of how to live well on far less than anyone had previously imagined was possible and still have a whale of a time doing it.

Tony and Faith grew vegetables, fruit and joy for several years before a National Park helicopter spotted a single solar panel glinting in the sunlight. A massive planning fight ensued, rallying huge numbers of local people into action, who occupied the house and prevented a JCB from demolishing what was evidently a perfectly comfortable home. Quick to spot the political tide turning against them, the Park then backed rapidly off. Tony has written one of the best selling books on sustainable housing, and is known all over the world for his particular kind of constructional technique.

Across the fields from Tony and Faith one enters a pleasant woodland. Only the traces of a worn footpath offers a clue that people live here, indeed most happily and successfully amongst this woodland. Several turf-roofed round houses have been erected here, under the watchful eyes of Emma Orbach, a totally dedicated pioneer in this kind of living and a woman with a mission to restore the kind of spiritual life that once flourished here prior to the decline of Druidism and Celtic Christianity. Emma and her husband Julian originally bought Brithdir Mawr and founded a community there before Emma decided to take matters a step further and live as close to nature as possible. There are echoes of the life of St Brynach running through all of her spiritual journey.

Similarly hounded by the planning authorities, the Pembrokeshire National Park and other regulatory bodies, Emma eventually obtained the planning needed to set up her spiritual community in the forest underneath Brithdir Mawr, practically on the axis of the *vesica piscis*. Meanwhile, hundreds of people from all over the world have passed through this 'invisible college' of straw-bale roundhouses during the past ten years. The press have mounted an occasional offensive against the radical and alternative nature of activities there and yet have continuously failed in their attempt to ridicule what is emerging. The media, who feed the mass consciousness, were naturally unable to get to grips with what is happening in this space, yet it remains true that around the globe most people involved in the alternative movement know all about what goes on at Fachongle and Brithdir Mawr.

These places represent a pioneering generation of the new ecological and spiritual movement, where lofty talk gets replaced by practical action, and where sustainable truly means attaining a zero-carbon footprint. In England, only Glastonbury can be compared in attracting alternative people and ideas promoting New Age values with such intensity. The symbol of Glastonbury is ...the *vesica piscis*. It is everywhere one looks, at holy wells, on mosaic floors and throughout the Abbey. Glastonbury was the prime Christian powerpoint in Britain throughout the early Christian epoch and well into the late middle ages. For many centuries it *generated* Christianity in Britain.

Glastonbury and the Vesica Piscis

In 1968, the late John Michell, another radical traditionalist, wrote a best-selling book that was to become the flagship of the alternative and earth-mysteries movement. *The View over Atlantis* looked at all that had been lost from the earlier 'pagan' and druidic traditions of Britain. One of the diagrams in John's book was his discovery of a giant *vesica piscis* which had

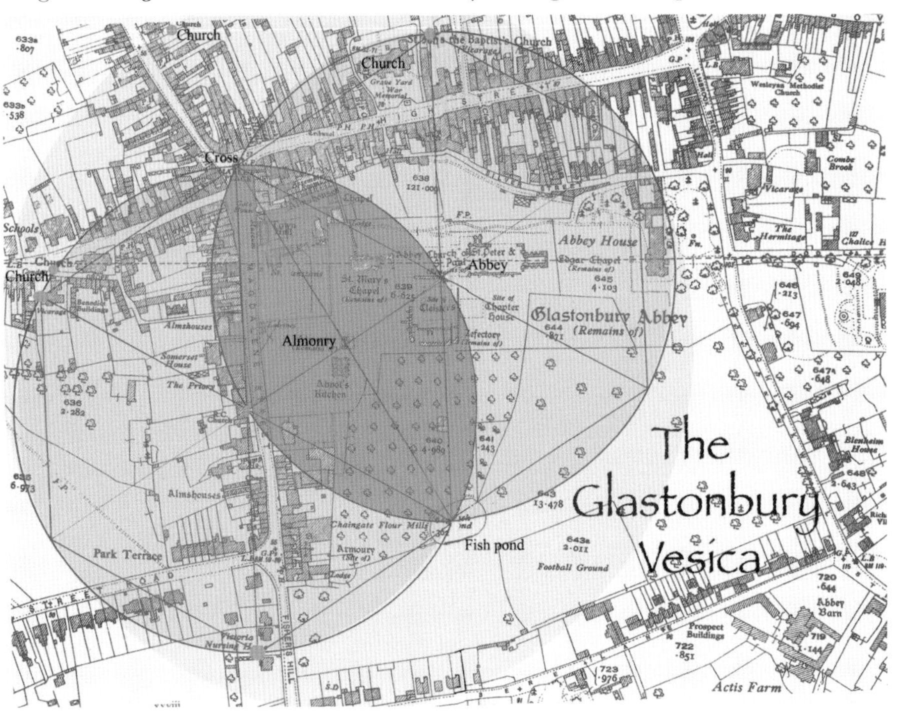

apparently influenced the layout of the town itself. Here the market cross with its large monolith replaces Nevern churchyard's bluestone cross. The Abbey replaces Pentre Ifan. The church conference centre stands in for Carningli, and the magnificent elliptical fishpond replaces Waun Mawn. All the churches in the town are located on the perimeter of the *vesica's* circles. Some monkish humour is suggested by the centre of this *vesica* being an almonry (almshouse) for the poor. So perfectly Christian to locate that there, while the word-play is *vesica* - mandorla(Italian for almond) - almonry.

Glastonbury hosts the largest music festival in Britain each year at the summer solstice, and an internationally famous children's festival each year. In the many bookshops are all the books one could ever read about alternative and spiritual ideas. The Abbey remains a holy hot-spot and pulls in dozens of coach loads of pilgrims and tourists while the Tor and the Chalice Well gardens hold a magical enchantment over all who visit them, perhaps partly because of the red and white chalybeate springs that separately flow from points only a few yards distant from each other, perhaps because the town is located on the St Michael line, and perhaps because the town is identified with the *vesica.*

Climate change has reinforced our belief that humans are affecting the landscape (environment). This material requires that one considers *that the landscape (environment) is affecting humans.* Today we do not understand this process at all well, but it appears that the megalith builders did.

A Vesica within Stone Circles

This book has focussed on finding evidence of prehistoric creativity. In the Preselis, and in other major regions of megalithic activity, it has been possible to demonstrate that creative ideas were evolving for understanding the cosmic patterns that create life on earth. Among the many designs that were used by this culture in achieving that goal were the curiously flattened circles, each based on the hexagonal (six-sided) geometry found in the *vesica piscis*. Thom named the two main designs he discovered the type A and the type B. The former is constructed by dividing a circle into six as one learns to do at school today, the latter by constructing a *vesica piscis*.

Both these two designs are found throughout northwestern Europe and the examples (*opposite*) are both from the English Lake District. They are very large, at 107 and 359 feet diameter, while the sole example of a flattened circle in the Preselis, a type B just above Glandy Cross, is only 28 feet in diameter and comprised of tiny stones. Essentially, and importantly, the geometry is identical whether large or small, and it is always based on a *vesica piscis*.

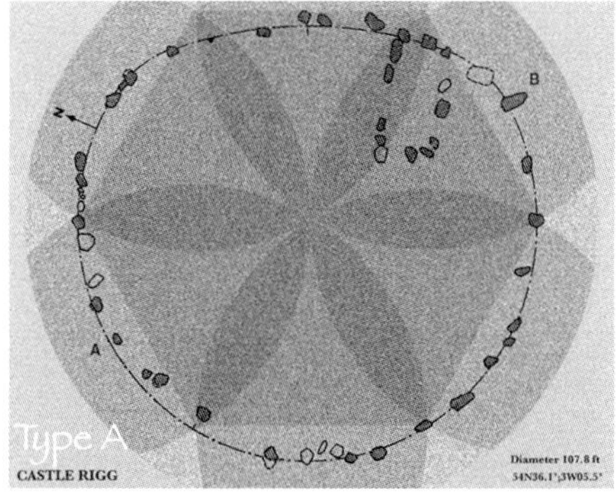

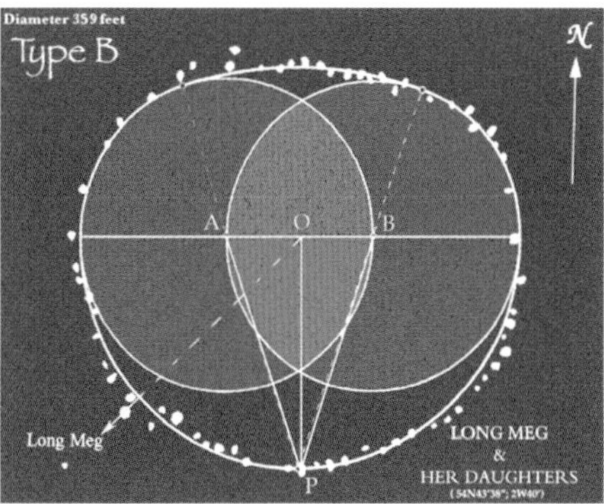

Megalithic flattened circle designs, the Type A (above) and type B (below), showing the constructional process, both based on hexagonal and vesica geometries.

The Lake District circles are thought by archaeologists to be among the oldest examples known, both Castle Rigg (*note that stones mark all six points of the hexagon*) and Long Meg were erected around 3200 BC. Pentre Ifan is dated at 3500 BC and this suggested to me that the Preseli *vesica* could have been part of a giant type B flattened circle across the landscape. The construction is simple enough, although the execution of the design on the landscape would not have been. However, the two *vesica* circles do not, in fact, need to be completed in order to complete the type B design. The perimeter and the finished design is shown in the lower illustration above.

I traced out the construction on my OS Map. A map of the arrangement is shown overleaf together with features, buildings and monuments that lie on the boundaries of the circles. The latter illustration will assist the reader in determining where the boundaries of this form are located. No interpretation is currently offered on the locations marked on the diagrams.

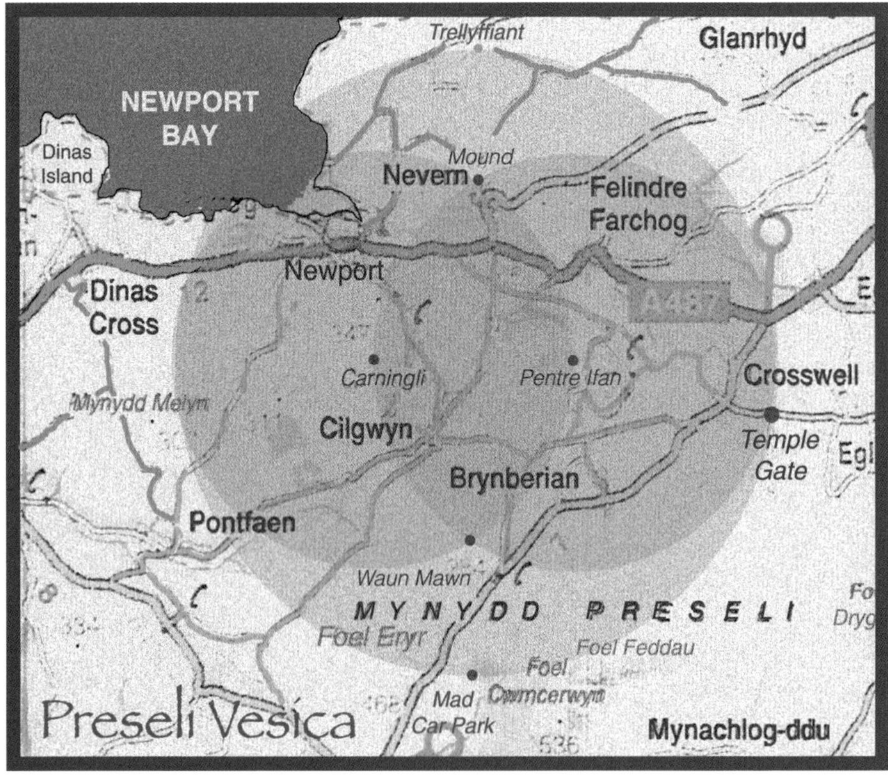

Two illustrations showing the extended vesica design as used in the construction geometry of neolithic flattened rings. The map above is included to orient and scale the design for the reader, the graphic opposite to provide finer details of monuments, farm names and other features.

A big treasure was to discover that the Trellyffiant dolmen and its outlier stone lie almost exactly on the northern boundary axis of the construction. There are other things of interest here too - many of the old 'Norman' farmsteads like Bayvil and Tregamman lie on the northern circumferences of these circles. Many buildings with 'carn' in their name are here, and Temple Gate takes the eastern boundary point, near Pontyglasier. Foel Eryr takes part in the construction. For the reader who has an OS map, placing a ruler between Nevern mound and Llech y Drybedd shows it to be the same distance

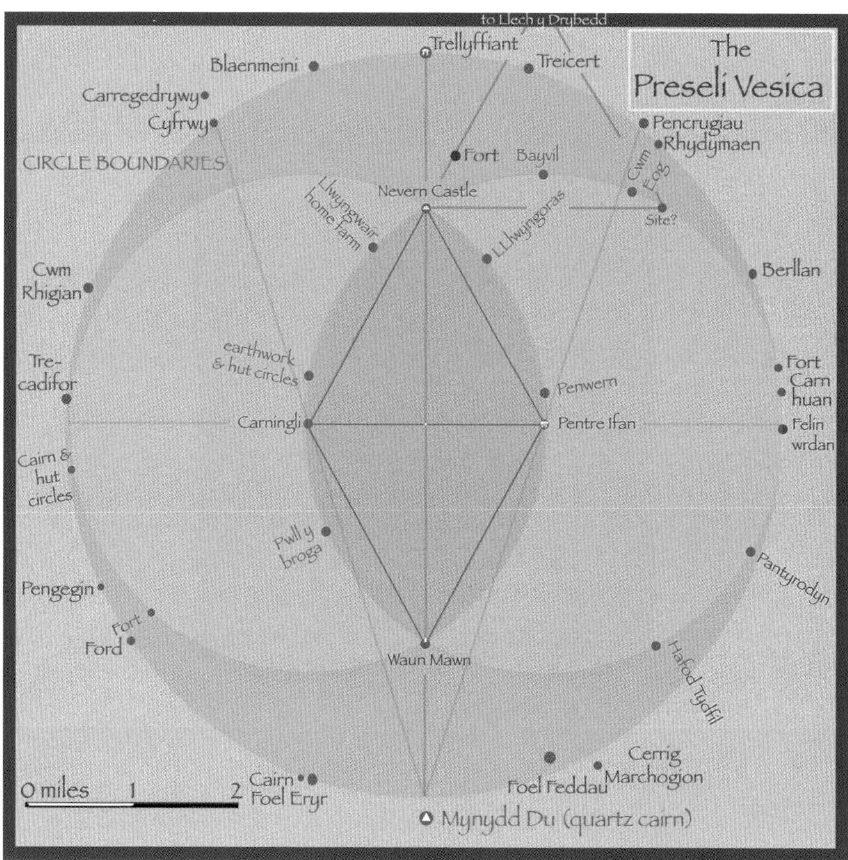

as the other triangle side lengths. The line is an extension from Carningli. Was this a grid of triangles - was there a site, now vanished, that terminated a little to the south-east of Cwm Eog? If there was, Llech y Drybedd would have provided the apex of a third triangle, Pentre Ifan a fourth. A fort, Castell Trefach (SN 087409) is located on the alignment from Carningli.

The southern point of the type B construction lies at the edge of a modern conifer plantation, at Mynydd Du. There is a large ruined quarz cairn here, located a few hundred feet south of the *vesica* perimeter. It falls on the north-south line through the axis of the whole construction.

Was the *vesica*, in any of the enlarged forms illustrated here, a reality? That must remain entirely up to the reader to assess. What is not in doubt is the accuracy of the placement of the four sites that form two back-to-back equilateral triangles, aligned to the cardinal points of the compass. That construction is a reality because it still exists, in hard stone, as does the extension to Llech y Drybedd. These sites are communicating with each other across the landscape, as have others described throughout this book.

This demonstrates that megalithic monuments are much more like verbs than nouns. They communicate in a kind of grammar or language which we can read only when we understand that language. Whether to the sun, moon, or to other monuments or natural features on the landscape, *geometry* has been shown to lie at the heart of it all, a language by which the world made sense to our prehistoric ancestors in their day; the same language by which it made sense to the Celtic Christian Church, and the same language which has enabled the megaliths to be decoded here, in our time. This language and this decoding can only be learned and applied through engaging with the sites themselves, by actually walking the landscape.

To affirm this continuity of function, and to demonstrate the need to understand geometry in any assessment of ancient artefacts, one need look no further than the inscribed Cross Stone now set into the window sill at Nevern church (*right*). Its loose and organic style belies the fact that the entire form is built around the geometry of the *vesica* and pythagorean triangles.

I therefore finish this story confident that the reader can now glean much more satisfaction from visiting megalithic sites than was previously possible and, having absorbed some of the methodology presented within in these pages, will be able to decipher more of these neglected 'dots' on the landscape, here and elsewhere, and thereby continue the task I have begun. That task is to reclaim our prehistoric heritage and, in so doing, to honour our ancestors.

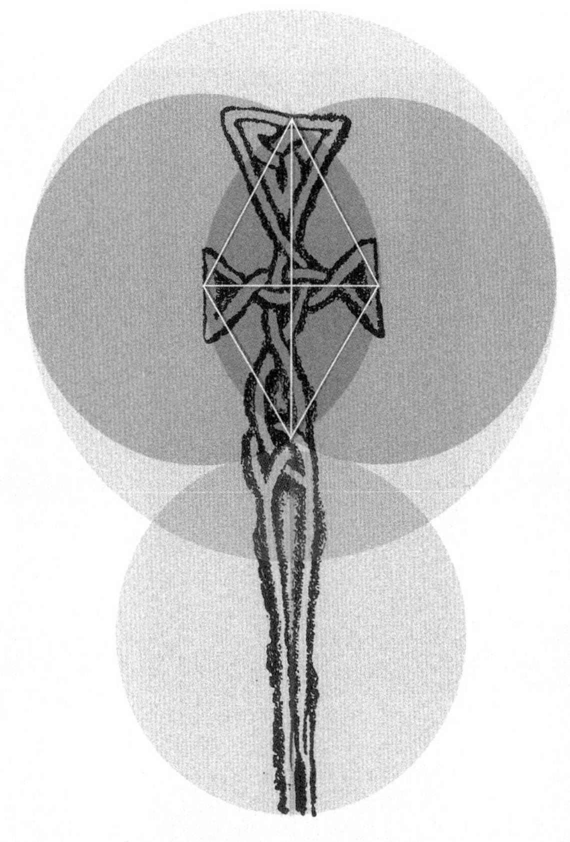

'Wonderful things' at Nevern

A Treasure in Nevern Church. The Cross Stone is presently set into a window sill in the southern chapel. A greatly admired and organic artwork, neither archaeologists nor Church historians have ever recognised that it is entirely constructed from the Sacred Geometry of the Vesica Piscis. The importance of Geometry in the Celtic Church is self-evident as is continuity of local prehistoric practices - Nevern Church lies directly under the Castle 'faery'mound and on the North point of the Preseli Vesica.

The inscribed cross is forty-eight inches by twelve inches, an identical rectangular ratio (4:1) to that of the lunation triangle and, in addition, the two 'side -arm' triangles are 'pythagorean' 3:4:5 triangles, also in units of one inch.

Finding out where the Sun & Moon will rise and set on any day.

If you are planning a visit to a site and want to know where the sun and moon will rise or set on the date of your visit, then you will need to find the azimuths (bearings) of rise and set. You will need a basic scientific calculator.

Look up the latitude of the site from a map or Google Earth, plus the declination of the sun and moon for that date from an almanac or website. Then, apply the following formula to discover where on the horizon they will rise and set.

For a level horizon, $$\text{Cos (Azimuth)} = \frac{\text{Sin(Declination)}}{\text{Cos (Latitude)}}$$

Example One. Find the sunrise position difference difference between Summer solstice declination in 2010 (+23.433°), and 3000 BC (+24.03°)

[Answer is 50.564° - 49.49° = 1.072°

Example Two. Stonehenge is at latitude 52.178*. A visit is planned for August 23rd. The sun declination (from tables) is + 11.55*. The plus sign lets us know that rises and sets will take place in the northern half of the sky.

Sin(Dec) = 0.2002 ; Cos(Lat) = 0.6269 Thus Cos (Az) = 0.2002/0.6269 = 0.3194

and cos -1(Az) = 71.374 degrees

The formula gives the azimuth of sunrise on August 23rd 2010 as **71.374 degrees.**

As all the angles of rise and set are symmetrical around an east-west line, then sunset azimuth will be 360 - 71.374 degrees = **288.625 degrees**

For the same date the moon declination is given as - 14.96 degrees. The minus sign tells us that the rise and set will be in the southern half of the sky. The sums take care of this and azimuth of moonrise and moonset at Stonehenge are calculated as 114.317 and 245.383 degrees respectively.

The set of the sun and the rise of the moon are almost 180 degrees apart, opposite each other, which tells us that a full moon is imminent (24th August 2010).

In practice these are close but approximate figures, as horizons are rarely level and there will be refraction and parallax to account for. If the horizon is a long way from the site the earth's curvature must also be factored in.

The all singing formula is $$\text{Cos (Az)} = \frac{\sin(\text{dec}) - \sin(\text{lat}) \times \sin(h)}{\cos(\text{lat}) \times \cos(h)}$$

where h = (horizon altitude) - (correction for earth's curvature) + (parallax) - (refraction)

For more information on techniques, tools and calculations, visit www.skyandlandscape.com

If the horizon altitude has been measured directly on site with a theodolite or clinometer, then the correction for the earth's curvature has already been accounted for and may be ignored in the formula.
Correction for earth's curvature = 0.0045 degrees per Km distance
Parallax = 0.002 for the sun and 0.95 for the moon
Refraction varies but for a level horizon averages 0.55 degrees.
A graphical table for finding the typical refraction value is given below:

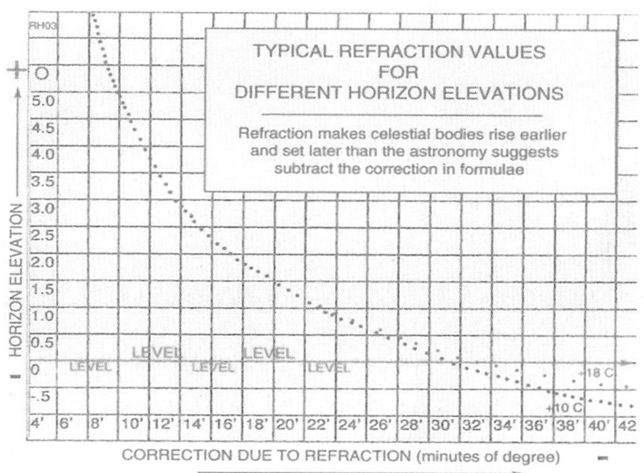

Landscape Geometry – Finding the Distance between Two Locations

Find the latitude and longitude difference separating each location A and B. A degree of latitude is 69.12 miles, a degree of longitude is 69.17 x cos(Mean Latitude) miles. Find the latitude and longitude distances and then apply this formula:

$$\text{Distance} = \sqrt{(\text{Latitude Distance B-A})^2 + (\text{Longitude Distance (B-A})^2}$$

The azimuth angle between the sites is:

$$\text{Azimuth} = \tan^{-1}(\text{Longitude Distance B-A})^2 \ / \ (\text{Latitude Distance (B-A})^2$$

If the Heights of the two locations are known, then the angle of dip or elevation will be given by:

$$\text{Dip or elevation angle} = \tan^{-1}(\text{Height difference/Distance apart})$$

These formulae are fine up to 50 miles, after which spherical geometry must be applied.

Using Compass, OS maps, Google Earth and GPS devices

For landscape work it may be useful to understand the following:

1. **The most commonly met error in landscape work is an assumption that the blue grid squares on an OS map align to the cardinal points of the compass**. They do not. Drawing up North-South or East-West lines on Ordnance Survey maps requires that you refer to the longitude printed around the top and bottom edges of the map, (for East-West lines use the latitudes on the right and left edges) from which North-South and East-West lines may then accurately be drawn onto the map. Large scale maps emphasize this distortion to the level where most people think that Liverpool or Cardiff lie West of Edinburgh. They do not.

2. **There is no substitute for visiting the site**. Landscape work must eventually move from mapwork to the landscape itself. Why? Because modern OS maps take liberties with where they mark the location of sites. Secondly, when at the site, a GPS reading will establish the latitude and longitude (and altitude above mean sea level) often to within 20 feet, which is much better than can be achieved easily from maps.

3. **OS grid references refer to an area square and not to a single point**. Therefore it is better to set up the GPS to read degrees, minutes and decimal fractions of a degree. Set the internal set-up of the GPS to OSGB, to correlate OS maps to the GPS's readings. With the display reading DD MM.DDD resolution down to 15 feet accuracy of a location is obtained. DD.MM.SS only resolves to a second, which is about 100 feet. Always record the elevation of a site. This often takes a few minutes to settle down on a GPS, but it makes issues with intervisibility between sites much easier to resolve if you recorded the elevation of each site and you are back at home 100 miles away!

4. **If you use Google Earth, the indicated latitude and longitude will be slightly different from those on an OS map**, and you will need to convert from WGS84 (Google's) to OGB36 (OS). The website www.nearby.org.uk does this (and will also convert a grid reference to lat/long, with OSGB being displayed below the WGS84 reading). Google Earth is useful for indicating distances between sites although not always as accurately as GPS readings taken on site.

5. **Determining direction**. The magnetic compass is best regarded only as a very rough guide to estimate direction in this type of work. The geology of Wales varies the compass reading, sometimes even reversing it! Much better is to use a GPS. To measure angles from a site, walk and peg a line of constant longitude (north-south) or latitude (east-west). Fix a cloth tape between the pegs, which realistically needs to be longer than a hundred feet. Use a large protractor to estimate other angles, for example to a prominent site on a distant horizon. Alternatively, apply the formulae on page 175.

6. **A theodolite is the ultimate tool for archaeoastronomy work** Save up the pennies and buy a secondhand one that does not invert the image.

£14.99

£12.99

Books by Robin Heath

PUBLISHED BY BLUESTONE PRESS

Purchasing enquiries:- bluestonepress@skyhenge.demon.co.uk

£12.99

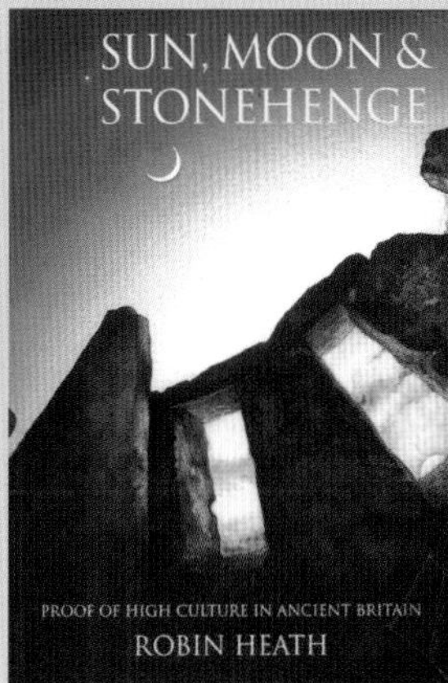

£9.95

Recommended Media Sources

Archaeoastronomy

A BBC 'Chronicle' Documentary: For a first class documentary about the pioneering work done by Professor Alexander Thom, you cannot better the BBC 1970 Chronicle programme, '*Cracking the Stone Age Code*', presented by the brilliant Magnus Magnussen. It is also a time-slice of post-war archaeological thinking. Richard Atkinson made a programme in this series about the dig he undertook at Silbury Hill.
www.bbc.co.uk/archive/chronicle/8604.shtml

Technical and research papers:

www.skyandlandscape.com
www.astro-archaeology.org

Map & Geodetic data:

www.nearby.org.uk

Site information:

www.themodernantiquarian.com
www.megalithic.co.uk
www.cadw.wales.gov.uk
www.stonepages.com
www.thatroundhouse.info (Tony Wrench's website)

Books:

The Secret Land. Paul Broadhurst with Robin Heath. Mythos Press. 2009

Neolithic Sites of Cardiganshire, Carmarthenshire & Pembrokeshire. George Children & George Nash. Logaston Press, 1997

A Book of Coincidence. John Martineau - Wooden books. www.woodenbooks.com

Sacred Geometry. Miranda Lundy - Wooden Books. www.woodenbooks.com

Practical Self-Sufficiency. John & Sally Seymour (1970s & various reprints).

Books by John Michell, Hamish Miller, Paul Broadhurst, Chris Street, Robert Lawlor, Tom Graves, Paul Devereux, Nicholas Mann, Laurence Main, John Sharkey, Nigel Pennick, Alfred Watkins, and Dillwyn Miles can be generally recommended to assist in this subject area.

EVENTS:

Megalithomania. Weekend Conference & Tours held during early May in Glastonbury. www.megalithomania. co.uk. Many good secondhand books available in the town!

Index

A

B

C

D

E

F

G

T

V

W

Y

Z

Bluestone Magic was researched, written, printed and published in Wales
and is a free-range, organic and sustaining resource